WISDOM from the ANCIENTS

◆

Bryan M. Litfin

HARVEST HOUSE PUBLISHERS
EUGENE, OREGON

Cover by Charles Brock

Interior design by KUHN Design Group

Cover photo © Taddeus, Wirestock / Depositphotos; mountainpix / Shutterstock; Wikimedia Commons (this image is in the public domain with unknown authorship)

For bulk, special sales, or ministry purchases, please call 1-800-547-8979.
Email: Customerservice@hhpbooks.com

M is a federally registered trademark of the Hawkins Children's LLC. Harvest House Publishers, Inc., is the exclusive licensee of the trademark.

Wisdom from the Ancients
Copyright © 2022 by Bryan M. Litfin
Published by Harvest House Publishers
Eugene, Oregon 97408
www.harvesthousepublishers.com

ISBN 978-0-7369-8462-1 (pbk.)
ISBN 978-0-7369-8463-8 (eBook)

Library of Congress Control Number: 2021937937

Printed in the United States of America

21 22 23 24 25 26 27 28 29 30 / BP / 10 9 8 7 6 5 4 3 2 1

Contents

Introduction

For better or worse, the lessons you learn from your parents stick with you for the rest of your life. Perhaps your parents did a great job. Or maybe not. They might have been a total bust. Probably, they were somewhere in between. If I had to guess I'd imagine your mom wasn't Mary Bailey from *It's a Wonderful Life*, but neither was she Cruella de Vil from *101 Dalmatians*. Your father was probably better than Luke Skywalker's, but not quite as good as Beaver Cleaver's. Am I right? Whoever they were, your parents surely taught you some unforgettable lessons.

My dad taught me two important things when I got my first job. Back in the 1970s, people still had their newspapers delivered by kids on bicycles. In Dallas, Texas, where I grew up, there were two daily papers. I delivered the afternoon paper: the *Dallas Times Herald*. On weekdays, I would roll them up and secure them with a rubber band, or maybe put a plastic bag around the rolls if it was a rainy day. The Sunday paper was a different story. Those thick slabs of wood pulp filled the canvas bag on my handlebars as if someone had poured concrete in there. Sometimes I had to deliver half the Sunday papers, pedal home to get the rest, then ride out again with the second batch.

One of the lessons my dad taught me was a lifelong nugget I've never forgotten. The other was the exact opposite of what he intended, but it was a good lesson nonetheless. The positive lesson was: "Son, go the extra mile with your customers. Make sure you throw the paper onto the porch." According to my boss at the *Times Herald*, it was sufficient to heave the newspaper onto the front lawn in the porch's general vicinity. But my dad taught me to put it right at the doorstep. If I missed the porch, I would stop, go back, and set it there. I received no extra reward for this. I was just doing the job to the best of my abilities. Exceeding expectations. Going the extra mile. Very wise advice from my dad!

The other lesson, which I still believe today, is to invest in excellent equipment to do the job right. Unfortunately I had to learn the hard way that what might seem like clever thriftiness can come back and bite you in the rear—literally! My dad and I found an old bike frame that had been dumped in the creek at the end of our street. We spray painted it, oiled the chain, and bought a new seat, handlebar grips, and tires. It looked great! That is, until you tried to ride it. I can still remember its wobbliness under the heavy load of the Sunday edition. Sometimes the handlebars would fall forward and spill my papers everywhere. After struggling to finish my paper route on those days, I'm convinced my makeshift bike's hard rubber seat actually did bite my rear a few times. I should have invested in a groovy 1970s BMX bike like all my friends had. Live and learn.

In this book you'll meet some spiritual mothers and fathers who have important lessons to teach us as well. There is great wisdom in listening to the previous ages. We need to learn the lessons of history lest we miss out on a blessing, or, as the saying goes, be doomed to repeat our mistakes. But to do this requires humility. Americans in particular tend to think of the future as the best place to cast our eyes. The next best thing is always around the corner. Yet as Christians, we have to be humble enough to pay attention to our ancestors and not always be looking ahead. Think about how much history the Bible records, both in the Old and the New Testament. Surely God wants us to learn from it! Hebrews 12:1 reminds us that there is a "cloud of witnesses" who ran the race before us. Shouldn't their experience on the racetrack of life give us something valuable?

When it comes to church history, each generation has something important to pass on. But the part of history I want to emphasize in this book is the ancient church period. We can also refer to it as the "early church" or the era of the "church fathers."[1] This historical era goes beyond the New Testament period—beyond the age of the original apostles. As you probably know, those first apostolic Christians lived and wrote and evangelized in the Roman Empire of the first century AD. But Christianity, of course, continued into the second, third, fourth, and fifth centuries and beyond.

Then, around AD 500, the empire of Rome fell to barbarian invaders. At that time church history made a pivot into the so-called Middle Ages (the ages between antiquity and the modern era). This book will focus only on the first 500 years after the birth of Christ—the ancient Greco-Roman world. Many great Christians lived in that foundational era about 70 generations ago. So please let me invite you to sit at the feet of your godly great-great-great (and so on) grandparents. I promise these ancients have much wisdom to pass on.

But to really gain something from these ancient lessons, you'll have to be willing to set aside your preconceived notions. You'll have to decide to be open-minded, to think outside the box. When I used to teach undergraduate theology, I would sometimes come to the first day of class with a stack of cups. I would set them on a table before those freshmen, who had been high schoolers until just that May. But now, in August, they were timid Bible college students. (Actually, some of them weren't timid, but rather cocky. They needed my lesson even more.) In front of the watching students, all of whom were at a major life transition, I would set the cups on the table, one by one, upside-down. "These cups represent doctrines," I would tell the expectant freshmen, "and *this* is the main thing you need to know to learn theology"—and then with a sweep of my arm, I would knock all the cups onto the floor. "A clean slate," I declared.

The lesson didn't end there. I would immediately bend down and

---

1. Although most ancient writers were men, certainly there were some wise church mothers as well. But for the purposes of this book I will use *church fathers* as a collective term for all the writers of this era.

pick up most (but not all) of the cups and replace them on the table. Unlike a secular university professor, I wasn't trying to break down the Christian beliefs of my students. My goal wasn't to deconstruct their faith into little bits, leaving these young people spiritually barren and nihilistic. No, I just wanted them to *own* what was on the table. I wanted their doctrines to be there on purpose. You see, it's one thing to accept what has always been part of your Christian upbringing without thinking about it. It's much different to put the cups back on the table after having wiped the slate clean. Then they're truly *your* cups. You chose to put them there. And the wise person will realize that a few of those cups probably shouldn't have been there in the first place. The trick is knowing which ones to leave on the floor.

Let me say at the outset that some of what you encounter in this book might sound startling. Perhaps you flipped through the table of contents and thought, *I don't agree with that, or that, or that. And hey! That one's heresy!* Please understand: My goal isn't to be provocative. This book isn't trying to be edgy just to be edgy. My only desire is to get you thinking in new ways about old topics. I want to put you in touch with the past so you can gain insight for the future. So go ahead; dig into the chapters—even the "heretical" ones—and I think you'll see what I mean. My prayer is that these insights are wise, useful, and biblically based. You might not agree with all my interpretations of the ancient fathers. That's fine. An open-minded learner can gain just as much from disagreeing with someone as from agreeing with them.

Some of what you read here might sound like Roman Catholicism. Perhaps you might think that's my starting point. Not at all. I am an evangelical, born-again Christian, and I desire to be nothing else. Therefore, my advice is to put Roman Catholicism out of your mind. The early Christians belonged to the little-c catholic church (that is, the "universal" or "whole" church), but they weren't Roman Catholics as we think of that term today. This book does not try to engage with Protestant-Catholic debates that happened a thousand years after the ancient period had ended. I have no desire to be anachronistic, to force a modern Christian mind-set back onto ancient times. The point is to go the other way—to let the views of the church fathers come forward, not inject our own views backward.

In this book I want to help you think like your spiritual ancestors thought and to learn from them if you can. Maybe we'll see that some of the things found in modern Roman Catholicism have their roots in ancient wisdom. And maybe you'll realize that some of the things we think are "essential" to Christianity actually come straight from modern Western views—but we can't see it because we're on the inside, like the goldfish in the bowl that doesn't realize it's wet. This is precisely why it helps to look back to the ancient times, before Protestants and Roman Catholics became divided in the 1500s. The ancient church fathers can give us a window into what earliest Christianity looked like before so many centuries had passed, before the faith had even left the Roman Empire in which it was born. There is so much to be gained from a backward glance like that—but only if you're willing to receive it. If you are, turn the page and let the wisdom of the ancients be their lasting gift to you.

1

The Cross of Christ Isn't Enough for Salvation

H ere is an exercise I've used with my theology students over the years. It's a little bit tricky, but at the same time, I find it very illuminating. Let's see if it tricks you too.

Imagine an unbelieving friend of yours wants to convert to Christianity. Knowing that you're a Christian, the person asks, "What must I do to be saved?" And let's imagine you reply like this. You say, "My dear friend, you first need to know that everyone is a sinner. Not just you, but everyone. We all fell into sin when our forefather Adam sinned. Therefore we all need a Savior, since we can't reach God through good deeds. No amount of human good works would be enough to earn God's favor. But thankfully God has provided a Savior for us! His love for his creatures is so great that he sent his only Son, who is fully God, to come to earth and become incarnate as a true man. Jesus committed no sin but was crucified on a Roman cross on our behalf. His death on the cross is a substitute that pays the divine price that our sinfulness demands. Whoever places their faith in Jesus Christ alone, trusting his death on the cross to take the place of the penalty we owe, will have eternal life. All you have to do is believe by faith in Jesus' atoning work and you will spend eternity with God. You will not be judged guilty because the shed blood of Christ covers you. The way to heaven is by faith alone. So, my dear friend, would you like to put your faith in Christ's finished work at the cross?"

"Yes!" your friend replies with great joy.

And you just sent that person to hell.

Now before you throw down this book, hear me out. I'm not a heretic—unless you think the apostle Paul is a heretic too. I will let him speak for me: "If Christ has not been raised, your faith is futile; you are still in your sins" (1 Corinthians 15:17). At no point in my so-called gospel proclamation did I ever mention the resurrection! I left Jesus on the cross, dying there as a substitute without conquering death, bursting from the tomb, and offering resurrection life to his followers. I emphasized the defeat of Good Friday but never mentioned the victory of Easter. It's a false gospel. Without the resurrection, "your faith is futile." And that is something no ancient Christian ever would have missed.

The Two-Word Gospel

The ancient church could—and often did—summarize the gospel in only two words: "Jesus is Lord." Now if you are a stickler for such things, you are probably thinking, *Come on, Litfin, that's three words.* Fair enough. But in Greek the expression was *Kyrios Iēsous*, with the "is" implied. *Kyrios* means "Lord," and I think you can recognize the second word. This was a triumphant proclamation, a Christian victory cry. The church fathers were saying, "No matter what you might think, you demons, you idols, you caesars with all your soldiers, in reality, Jesus is Lord!"

Can you hear the rejoicing in their voices? Can you feel their sense of release from bondage to pagan religion? This ancient expression is layered with so much more meaning than we might see at first. We are so accustomed to hearing about the "Lord Jesus" that we don't easily recognize all that this title implies. But the early Christians couldn't help but hear the Old Testament as they confessed Jesus' lordship with rich overtones of deity and exaltation. The Hebrew name for God, *Yahweh*, was never uttered by the Jews. Instead, they said *Adonai*, or Lord. And in the Greek version of the Old Testament, known as the

Septuagint, the translation of *Adonai* was *Kyrios*. So when you hailed Jesus as Lord in the ancient church, you were associating him with the glory of the one true God. The early and enthusiastic use of this expression is one of the main proofs that Jesus was worshiped as divine right from the beginning of Christianity.

Why was Jesus recognized as Lord? Because of his resurrection. After he rose from the dead, the lordship of Christ took on new meaning. The interesting thing about *kyrios* is that it can sometimes be a rather plain term. It can mean "sir," like you'd call some respectable man you might meet on the street; or "master," like a slave would say to his owner. With this more common nuance, the word was applied to Jesus as the disciples' master. However, once he rose from the dead, the disciples realized who Jesus really was: not just a mighty prophet but God in the flesh. Think of what the disciple Thomas exclaimed when he came face to face—and finger to wound—with the risen Christ. "My Lord and my God!" he cried in wonder (John 20:28). And when Peter was preaching the risen Christ to the Jews, he said, "God has made him both Lord and Christ, this Jesus whom you crucified" (Acts 2:36 ESV). The Messiah's deity and his victorious resurrection were handily summarized in the expression, "Jesus is Lord."

Have you ever recited the Apostles' Creed? We will talk about creeds in a future chapter, but allow me to mention one thing now. Jesus is called "Lord" in that creed. Over time, the creeds we know today expanded from early tidbits of apostolic preaching, like Peter's preaching in Acts 2. At the very core of this message was the triumphant proclamation, "Jesus is Lord." Such glorious truth was supposed to be uttered aloud. That is why the apostle Paul said in Romans 10:9, "If you declare with your mouth, 'Jesus is Lord,' and believe in your heart that God raised him from the dead, you will be saved." Do you see? The resurrection is the heart of the gospel. It is the essence of what Christians must say and believe in order to be saved. From this primitive confession, the creeds gradually expanded to include even more content about God, the works of Jesus, the Holy Spirit, and the church. But at the fountainhead of early Christian belief was the lordship of Christ based on his empty tomb and exaltation to the Father's right hand.

The declaration that Jesus is Lord also made clear who isn't deserving of that title. The early believers knew that the rulers of Rome claimed lordship as well. Increasingly, the emperors began to accept divine titles, even worship. Temples and idols to their imperial majesty sprang up across the landscape. Every citizen with a coin in his palm was holding a miniature idol that celebrated the glory of Rome and the demonic spirits that inspired its leaders. Ancient Rome demanded total lordship. The emperor was the earthly embodiment of divine power. Christians who refused to honor this false god could be killed.

In the year AD 156, a man named Polycarp, bishop of Smyrna, stood before a judge in an arena filled with pagans ravenously calling for his blood. The judge ordered Polycarp to offer incense and swear an oath to the demonic power of Emperor Antoninus Pius. "What harm is there in saying, 'Caesar is Lord'?" the judge asked him. But Polycarp's famous answer was, "For eighty-six years I have served Christ, and he has done me no wrong. How could I now blaspheme my King who saved me?"[1] Upon making this courageous reply, Polycarp went to the flames with boldness and eternal hope. It was yet another example of what Acts 17:7 had recorded: "They are all defying Caesar's decrees, saying that there is another king, one called Jesus." The ancient Christians rejoiced that the Roman Empire—with its brutal government and foul gods—no longer held them in bondage. The risen Christ had crushed his enemies underfoot. He alone was victorious!

The Cross and the Crown

As my tricky illustration above revealed, modern Christians can so easily focus on the cross that the resurrection gets overlooked. None of us intends to exclude the empty tomb from our gospel proclamation. The cross just seems so important! And of course it is. Yet we too often forget, except for one day a year, to repeat the angel's words, "He is not here; he has risen, just as he said" (Matthew 28:6).

Unlike us, the early church always put the resurrection front and

---

1. *Martyrdom of Polycarp* 9.3, translation mine.

center. One reason for this difference is that the ancient Christians experienced crucifixion more vividly than we do. They were much closer to its hideous realities. A cross was no mere symbol for them. Many of them would have seen, or at least heard stories of, those naked and bloody victims writhing in agony and gasping for air while impaled on wooden stakes. For the ancient Christians, Jesus' crucifixion couldn't be the main focus of the story. That would imply the story had ended in tragedy and defeat. But thanks be to God, it didn't!

Now, for sure, the cross was proclaimed in the ancient church. Those first believers didn't shut their eyes to its horrors. In fact, the written manuscripts of their Scriptures often drew a little picture of a crucified man whenever the word "cross" or "crucify" was used.[2] Archaeologists have even found a mocking piece of graffiti that somebody scrawled on a Roman bedroom wall. It shows Jesus upon the cross with the head of a donkey, while a man named Alexamenos worships his seemingly foolish God. Clearly, the early Christians were known—and scorned—for revering a crucified Messiah. Yet they always emphasized that while Rome had killed their Lord, he had overcome the grave and offered eternal life to his followers.

Christ the Victor

In historical theology, this emphasis on victory is called the *Christus Victor* motif. Various understandings of Christ's atonement have emerged at different eras in church history. Sometimes one theme came to be widely celebrated, while at other times a different facet of Christ's work was the most emphasized. The ancient fathers certainly understood that the cross was a substitutionary sacrifice that paid a price in blood. Isaiah 53 and the book of Hebrews had made that clear. Yet the early Christian view of salvation didn't emphasize a law court in which a judge demanded a penalty and Jesus paid the price in our place. Rather, the ancients felt the weight of the fearsome idols that

---

2. The figure, called the staurogram, was formed from the Greek letters *tau* and *rho* superimposed to make the shape: ⳨.

surrounded them, the government that oppressed them, the grave that beckoned for them, and the devil who tempted them. In the face of such dangers, the earliest believers rejoiced that these terrible chains had been shattered when the stone was rolled away at Easter's dawn.

Do you want to know how the ancient Christians pictured this great truth in their art? They didn't draw an old rugged cross on a hill, or a grave in a hillside with its round stone ajar. Rather, they depicted three scenes from the life of the biblical prophet Jonah. In the first scene, Jonah was shown being swallowed by a sea monster that represented the chaotic and deadly underworld, the abyss from which no one returns. But just like Jonah was ejected from the fish after three days, Jesus returned from the grave after three days! (Matthew 12:39–41) So the second scene was Jonah bursting from the sea monster's mouth, while the third was Jonah resting under a vine in the garden of Paradise. There are many depictions of this sequence on the walls of the ancient catacombs and on marble coffins. Perhaps closer to home, the Cleveland Museum of Art owns a set of beautiful Christian statues that depict the same scenes. These were visual reminders not to fear death, since the grave would one day give up its dead and the believer in Christ would reign in heaven forever.

The early Christians knew that death and Satan haunted their footsteps. The devil's power was personified by Rome and its gods. The demons were real, and they would hurt you if they could. Previous generations had lived in dread of this occult power all around them. But no more! The enemy was defeated. Death had lost its sting. Jesus Christ was alive. The magnificent truth that the ancients emphasized is just as glorious for us as it was for them: He is risen!

And all God's people said?

He is risen indeed.

> *"Where, O death, is your victory? Where, O death, is your sting?"*
> *The sting of death is sin, and the power of sin is the law.*
> *But thanks be to God!*
> *He gives us the victory through our Lord Jesus Christ.*
>
> 1 Corinthians 15:55-57

2

Weakness Is the Best Witness

A llow me to introduce you to an ancient man named Pudens. He was a real man, not a figure from legend. Pudens appears only briefly in a famous story called *The Passion of Saints Perpetua and Felicity*, one of the most gripping and beloved martyr stories to come down to us from the ancient church.

Pudens was a Roman army officer who served as the prison warden in the city of Carthage. Two hundred years after the birth of Christ, a persecution broke out in that African city, and some believers were rounded up for interrogation and possible execution. The most prominent of them was Perpetua, a noblewoman about 22 years old. Imprisoned with her in the gloomy dungeon were friends including her handmaiden, Felicity, and her spiritual mentor, Saturus.

As the Christians suffered in the jail's hot and crowded conditions, and as they testified to their faith in Jesus under great pressure, their bravery caught the jailer's eye. The ancient text tells us that Pudens, a pagan man, began to honor the faithful believers because he discerned the spiritual power at work in them. He started to let other Christians visit their jailed brethren to encourage them.

We meet Pudens again on the day the martyrs died. All of them had been brought to the amphitheater of Carthage, whose stone ruins can still be visited in Tunisia today. The brave Christians Perpetua and

Felicity were cast before the crowd, entangled in nets, to be trampled by a mad cow. Their wise mentor Saturus, however, was unhurt by the wild boar that was supposed to gore him to death. In fact, it gored the handler instead!

Saturus was returned to the arena gate where Pudens was standing guard. To encourage the newly converted jailer, Saturus decided to describe the fulfillment of a prophecy. Earlier, he had predicted he would be cast before a leopard. "Watch and see," he said to Pudens, "I'm going back in there to be finished off by one bite of a leopard."[1]

And that was what happened. After one attack from the fierce cat, Saturus was so drenched in blood that the crowd mocked him with the typical greeting uttered at a spa: "Well washed!" But the Christians recognized this to be a different kind of washing—not the external cleansing of a Roman bath, but the "baptism of blood" predicted by Jesus. "Can you drink the cup I drink or be baptized with the baptism I am baptized with?" he had asked his disciples (Mark 10:38). Now the martyrs of Carthage were following in their Savior's bloody footsteps.

As Saturus lay bleeding to death from the leopard bite, Pudens knelt beside him. "Farewell," Saturus whispered with his dying breath. "Remember me and my faith. Don't let these things dismay you. Be strengthened instead!" Then Saturus did something strange: He asked Pudens for his finger ring. After dipping it in his own blood, Saturus handed it back as an "inheritance" and a "symbol and reminder of his bloody martyrdom."[2] Of all the martyrs who perished on that holy day, Saturus was the first to meet his Lord.

But what happened to Pudens? The ancient text tells us only that he became a believer, nothing more. However, another document has come down to us from the Carthaginian church. It lists the days on which to commemorate the saints and martyrs of ancient times. In that calendar, what name do you suppose is listed for April 29? A martyr named Pudens from the city of Carthage. Apparently, Pudens accepted

---

1. Bryan M. Litfin, *Early Christian Martyr Stories* (2014) 108.

2. Litfin, *Martyr Stories*, 108.

more than a golden ring that day from his admired brother Saturus. He accepted the first step on the road to martyrdom as well.

"The Christians to the Lions!"

If there's one mental image that modern people have of the ancient church, it's a handful of Christians in togas waiting piously while a lion advances to eat them. That scene has been depicted often in sacred art. The heroic stories have been told countless times for spiritual encouragement. Even Hollywood got into the act with the 1951 movie *Quo Vadis*. There's a scene in that film where Nero mocks the faithful believers and Peter rebukes him. Then the lions are let loose with a trumpet fanfare. Much roaring ensues from the cats as well as the crowd. But, of course, the Christians meet their fate with firm resolve.

While devotional piety often stretches the truth and Hollywood always takes its liberties, the events themselves are not pure fiction. Though persecutions didn't happen constantly, and martyrdom was not an everyday occurrence, they certainly did happen. And it wouldn't take more than once for your pastor to be tortured or a holy daughter of your church to be raped and martyred to make an indelible impression on your congregation.

Why did the Romans do this sort of thing? The social motivation behind Christian persecution was complex, and the reasons for it changed over the three centuries it happened to the ancient church. At the most basic level, it was all part of the Romans' bloodthirsty entertainment. The practice of watching gladiators fight to the death had been enjoyed since long before Christ was born. Another popular pastime in that era was watching hunters match their wits and spears against fierce beasts. Just as with violent movies of today, the producers of those ancient spectacles wanted to increase the body count and make sure a lot of blood got splashed around. What better way to do it than to toss some hated and defenseless criminals into the arena? And nobody was more hated in those days than the Christians.

Nevertheless, the church expanded rapidly despite these threats. After the apostolic age passed and Christianity grew in prominence in the second and third centuries, officials in the Roman government began to pay more attention to this strange, new faith. One governor named Pliny, who ruled over a province in modern-day Turkey, found himself uncertain when some church members were brought before him. Was Christianity a legal association or not? Were these people guilty of a crime just for being Christians? What did they actually do in their secret meetings? How were these weirdos supposed to be punished?

Pliny decided to get some advice from his boss in Rome, the emperor Trajan. A copy of the letter he wrote survives today. Pliny told Trajan that he'd tortured a couple of deaconesses for information and discovered that the Christians were relatively harmless. All they did was gather at dawn, sing hymns to a god named Jesus, commit themselves to a holy life, and share a regular meal together. Even so, Pliny pressured the Christians to recant. In particular, he urged them to curse the name of Jesus and worship idols of the emperor and the gods. Whoever complied, Pliny set free. But whoever did not, he executed. The point of Pliny's letter was to find out whether the emperor agreed with this plan.

Trajan wrote back, and his letter also survives. Trajan decreed that Pliny had done the right thing by executing the Christians. Of course, the government shouldn't go seeking them out, and the courts shouldn't pay attention to anonymous accusations which had no validity in Roman law. Yet when Christians were discovered, they should be put to a test. Whoever denied being a Christian anymore, and proved it by worshiping idols, should be let go without penalty. But if anyone persisted in claiming the name of Christ, that person must be punished.

The plan Trajan and his governor worked out in their letters became standard religious policy for many decades. Christians weren't sought out for destruction. However, if they somehow came to a governor's attention—as happened in AD 203 with Perpetua and her friends at Carthage—they had to recant or face the consequences. The governors had wide latitude to deal with the Christians as they saw fit, including the death penalty by decapitation, or worse, being torn apart as food for the savage beasts.

As the years went on, the church expanded even more and became prominent in every city. By the late third century, it was a widespread community whose leaders possessed noteworthy civic influence. In this same era, the emperor's power was starting to crumble and civil wars were threatening to shatter the Roman Empire into pieces. Some emperors got the idea that the only force that could truly reunify the empire was Rome's ancient devotion to its gods. Therefore, any competing religion like Christianity had to be destroyed.

Now the reactionary policy of Pliny and Trajan was changed to an active, empire-wide extermination. To prove loyalty to the state, the government demanded that every citizen obtain an affidavit stating they had worshiped the imperial gods. Many Christians capitulated to this demand under the threat of torture and death. But some did not. Christian blood began to redden the streets of Rome like never before.

The worst persecution of all began in the year 303. Emperor Diocletian, egged on by evil henchmen in his administration, decreed the total end of Christianity. He began to issue edicts of increasing severity. Brutal and twisted tortures were invented for the Christians, the victims publicly displayed to frighten the masses into submission. It was the darkest hour the church had ever faced.

Into all this chaos stepped the emperor who is most famous for converting to Christianity. Yet now isn't the time to tell his story. We will discuss the significance of Emperor Constantine in chapter 21. For now, we should focus our attention on the martyrs who stood strong in those hideous days of mayhem and death. Christians across the empire were being thrown before leopards and lions, bears and bulls. They were burnt, slashed, stabbed, and whipped. The savage onlookers, as bestial as the animals they watched, hungered for Christian blood to run into the sand.

One observer who witnessed these things was a Christian named Eusebius, the bishop of Caesarea in Palestine. Eusebius recorded the stories of the brave martyrs in his famous book, *Church History*. "What witness of these events was not astonished by the steadfastness of these utterly amazing champions of godliness under countless lashes? Or their struggle against man-eating beasts that immediately followed the whipping?" Eusebius watched these deaths not with the eyes of lust and cruelty, but with a spiritual perspective. "In that hour," he declared, "I could see the ever-present divine power from the One to whom they testified—our Savior Jesus Christ himself—clearly manifested in the martyrs!"[3]

The Blood of Christians Is Seed

What would it have been like to live through those days? Let us imagine an orphaned child who lost a mother or father to the Great Persecution. If that orphan grew up and lived to a ripe old age, he or she would have been alive in the year 380 when a momentous event occurred. In that year, Emperor Theodosius issued a decree commonly called the Edict of Thessalonica. This new imperial law made Christianity—including belief in the Trinity of Father, Son, and Holy Spirit—the official religion of the Roman Empire.[4] No longer were the pagan deities to be worshiped by the empire's citizenry. Soon, their idols and temples would be torn down. The gods and caesars of Rome had finally bowed the knee to the true Lord of the cosmos.

What mighty force converted this rapacious and violent empire to Christ? What kind of strength could bring the glory of Rome into submission? Did it happen like the days of the Crusaders, when iron-clad knights made their conquests with crosses upon their shields and infidel blood upon their swords?

Definitely not. No weaponry was deployed in this original fight except the sword of the Spirit, the shield of faith, and the full armor of God (Ephesians 6:13-17). And in this, the ancient church fathers teach us an amazing and counterintuitive truth: *Weakness is our best witness.* We won't convert unbelievers through fancy words and slick presentations. Although persuasive arguments do have their place in apologetics, in the end, we must back up our message with humble and courageous deeds lived out before the watching masses.

---

3. Litfin, *Martyr Stories*, 149.

4. Emperor Constantine is often attributed with making Christianity the empire's official religion, but that is mistaken. Constantine simply ended the persecution of Christians and gave them his full support (see chapter 21). Theodosius made Christianity the state religion and ordered the dismantling of old paganism.

In other words, the best way to catch the eye of unbelievers isn't by showing them the accomplishments of your pastor, the coolness of your church, or the "blessings" that Christians gain. You can't convince non-Christians to join God's side for the comfort and ease he will provide. Rather, what gets noticed by the watching world is your willingness to stay committed to your Lord even when society puts the screws on you and demands that you cave in. Such courage makes others want to join the Christian faith. That is what the church father Tertullian meant when he said, "The blood of Christians is seed."[5] The more you cut down Christians like stalks of wheat, sowing their blood in the sand, the more people will admire that determination and spring up to take their place. Or as Jesus put it, "unless a kernel of wheat falls to the ground and dies, it remains only a single seed. But if it dies, it produces many seeds" (John 12:24).

Of course, not everyone will honor your costly stand. Many will continue to jeer and ridicule—in fact, most will. Just like the mob that watched Saturus get torn open by a leopard, some people will celebrate the outpouring of Christian blood (in whatever form that might take). They will heap on you the same scorn that the soldiers cast upon Jesus himself. You will be called intolerant and foolish for being a devoted Christian.

Even so, mixed in among the mockers, there will always be a few who think differently. These people, moved by the Spirit of God, will take notice of your steadfast courage and be drawn to it. In the weakness of being downtrodden and despised, your perseverance will be admired. By taking such an undaunted stand for Christ, you too may find a Pudens who receives from your hand not a ring of bloody gold but the crown of eternal life.

For Christ's sake, I delight in weaknesses, in insults, in hardships, in persecutions, in difficulties. For when I am weak, then I am strong.

2 CORINTHIANS 12:10

---

5. *Apology* 50, translation mine.

◆ 3 ◆

Often, Our Biggest
Threats Look a Lot like Us

In the desert southwest of North America, there flies a noble bird called the zone-tailed hawk. Most of us who see a hawk soaring in the sky consider it a beautiful sight. But that sentiment isn't shared by the rabbits, mice, prairie dogs, and lizards that might be scurrying beneath the bird's watchful eyes. Those animals know to look upon a hawk with fear.

Turkey vultures, on the other hand, aren't scary at all. Small animals know, when they see their particular shape and flying pattern in the sky, that these birds don't present a predatory threat. Vultures eat carrion instead of preying on living things. So what does the clever zone-tailed hawk do? It has evolved to look and fly much like the harmless turkey vultures of its native habitat. The hawk mingles among the vultures as if he's just one of the crowd. Then, at an opportune moment, he swoops out of the flock and dives upon his prey. Although the hawk seemed perfectly harmless up there—just soaring like a vulture with no deadly intent—he was a killer all along. His sharp talons and rapacious beak make this all too clear to the unsuspecting rabbit or the quivering little mouse.

The principle of camouflage is an ancient one, and it isn't restricted to nature. It's also used in espionage. Would a CIA spy saunter down Moscow's streets wearing Levi's and cowboy boots, eating cheeseburgers and slurping Cokes, and speaking in a thick, Texas drawl? Of course not! The goal in espionage is to become a "gray man." This person is neither one thing nor the other, but only a drab character in the background. Nothing about him stands out. He wears nothing flashy and does nothing memorable. By blending into the crowd, he is able to move about the streets without generating alarm. Yet all the while he is an enemy agent working for a hostile government.

Believe it or not, the ancient church had infiltrators like this in their ranks. They weren't secret agents, but they were definitely outsiders who had snuck into the sheepfold without actually becoming one of the flock. Jesus spoke about such people in Matthew 7:15-20: "Watch out for false prophets," he warned. "They come to you in sheep's clothing, but inwardly they are ferocious wolves." This is the origin of the expression, "a wolf in sheep's clothing." Eventually, Jesus' word picture became a fable in which a wolf was able to sneak close to a flock of sheep by wearing a wooly disguise.

How does Jesus want us to recognize these false prophets? He switched to a tree metaphor to tell us: "By their fruit you will recognize them. Do people pick grapes from thornbushes, or figs from thistles? Likewise, every good tree bears good fruit, but a bad tree bears bad fruit…Every tree that does not bear good fruit is cut down and thrown into the fire. Thus, by their fruit you will recognize them." We learn something important here. Externally, all trees have the same basic features: roots, trunks, branches, leaves. But not all trees are equally profitable for humanity. The keeper of the orchard needs to recognize what kind of fruit each species of tree will produce. Some trees in ancient times gave good fruits, edible and healthy. Others produced bad fruits that were bitter or even poisonous. Jesus had no problem declaring that the bad apples were destined for hell. They will be "cut down" by God, he said, and be "thrown into the fire" (Matthew 7:19). Clearly, false doctrine is no small thing in the Lord's eyes!

Ancient Heresies

After Jesus ascended back to heaven, the meaning of his life and ministry became a topic of wide dispute among ancient people. Some

Christians held firm to what Jesus himself had taught and what the original apostles believed and communicated about him: that he was the Lord and Son of God who died for our sins and rose from the grave. But others made up fantastic stories about Jesus or interpreted him in their own free-thinking way. Sometimes they even put words in the Savior's mouth in their secret scriptures. A term came to be applied to such people: *heretics.* It comes from the Greek word for "choice." Heretics were those who chose to split away from the original truth so they could concoct new ideas about Jesus, even establishing their own independent sects.

Today we don't use the term *heretic* very often. It conjures up images of the medieval Inquisition, when Spanish clerics tortured heretics or even burned them at the stake. This is a terrible thing. Obviously, in a free and democratic society, people should have the right to believe whatever they want. The government shouldn't compel anyone to adopt a belief they don't want to, especially not by force.

However, that doesn't mean the Christian church shouldn't identify false teachers as heretics. The apostles certainly did. In 2 Timothy 3:6-8, Paul warned against the kind of people "who worm their way into homes and gain control over gullible women, who are loaded down with sins and are swayed by all kinds of evil desires, always learning but never able to come to a knowledge of the truth...They are men of depraved minds, who, as far as the faith is concerned, are rejected." The apostle Jude said the same thing in his New Testament epistle: "Certain individuals whose condemnation was written about long ago have secretly slipped in among you. They are ungodly people, who pervert the grace of our God into a license for immorality and deny Jesus Christ our only Sovereign and Lord" (1:4). Notice how the apostles didn't hold back their words of condemnation. Heretics are a clear and present danger to the Christian church. True believers ignore them at their own peril.

The False "Knowledge" of Heretics

During the ancient church period, there were many different heresies. Often the various sects overlapped in their beliefs. One large group of them had such similar teachings that historians refer to this collection of ideas as Gnosticism—a term that is hard to define with precise boundaries, yet has a clear ideological core. The Greek word *gnosis* means "knowledge." At the heart of this movement was the idea that salvation comes not from the death of Christ on the cross—which many of the Gnostics denied even happening—but from the secret knowledge that Jesus supposedly passed on to his disciples.

The Gnostic leaders claimed to be the recipients of Jesus' wisdom about salvation. They taught that humanity's problem isn't moral sin against a holy God. Rather, it is lack of understanding about the way the universe was formed, how the angelic beings function in it, and how people can access those spirits to achieve mystical unity with the highest power. Only the Gnostic teachers possessed this secret knowledge from Jesus. But if you joined their group, you could learn it too.

All this might sound like the beliefs of the lunatic fringe because it's so distant from what everybody agrees Christianity is about. But that wasn't the case in ancient times. Back then, the type of Christianity that focused on the death and resurrection of Jesus was in vigorous competition with the Gnostics, who claimed that real Christianity was their own knowledge-based version. The Gnostics ridiculed the ignorant believers who thought that Jesus died on a cross in a physical body, then returned to a body to save us from our sins. No, the Gnostics claimed, true Christianity is intangible and intellectual. Jesus' body was just a ghostly shape that he used to communicate with us. Our problem is lack of knowledge, and salvation consists of learning secrets about the cosmos from the elite few.

Gnosticism like this was more convincing to ancient people than you might think. At first glance, the Gnostics looked and sounded a lot like Christians because they talked so much about Jesus. They treasured his words and investigated their inner meaning. Many of them also led lives of respectable self-denial, separating themselves from the world and its attachments. So the people of the Roman Empire were confused. Which tree gives the good fruit and which the bad? Is that animal in the meadow a sheep? Or a wolf?

Fortunately, great Christian apologists rose up in the ancient church to defend the true faith. One of the foremost of them was Bishop Irenaeus of Lyon (today the second-largest city in France). Irenaeus wrote a five-volume work that is usually called *Against Heresies*, but whose full name was *Detection and Overthrow of What Is Falsely Called Knowledge*. Irenaeus's title alluded to Paul's exhortation in 1 Timothy 6:20, "Turn away from godless chatter and the opposing ideas of what is falsely called knowledge." Like Paul, Irenaeus recognized that godless busybodies would sneak into the church and claim to know the Lord's truth. But as Paul said in verse 21, these people have actually "departed from the faith."

The wide-ranging arguments of Irenaeus's masterwork are too lengthy to summarize here. At the core of it, though, was the notion of a *storyline*. Irenaeus insisted that the Gnostics didn't just have false doctrines. They were actually telling a completely different story about Jesus. In the true Christian narrative, he is the Son of God who was predicted by the prophets, born of a virgin, crucified by Pilate, and resurrected for the salvation of humankind. But the Gnostics used the same bits and pieces from the Bible to make up an entirely different myth. This would be, Irenaeus suggested, like taking a beautiful mosaic of a king, picking out all the jeweled pieces, and rearranging them to make a picture of a dog.[1] Sure, those were the same pieces. But that isn't the same image. Not at all. You've turned the king into something else.

Secret Knowledge or the Risen Christ?

From the first century through the third, two main views of Jesus—the Gnostic and the orthodox—competed for supremacy. (There were actually many perspectives about Jesus in antiquity, but these were the two largest and most visible ones.) Don't underestimate how attractive the Gnostic view was to the people of those times. To ancient ears, it sounded clever and intellectual. It offered a feeling of elitism, and it had many smart and persuasive leaders. Lots of people joined up with the Gnostics. The problem was, it wasn't real Christianity. It was a classic heresy. Yet how could this be known for sure?

---

1. *Against Heresies* 1.8.1.

The church fathers like Irenaeus encouraged their flocks to find the truth by identifying what was believed in the very beginning. A true Christian must adhere to the exact same storyline that the apostles started to preach as soon as their eyes left the ascended Christ. Although there could be many different nuances in the telling of that story—because many different communities did the telling—pretty soon the true believers began to realize that the common ground they shared was the incarnate, risen, and ascended Christ. As we saw in chapter 1, "Jesus is Lord" was the original confession of the early church. Here, then, was the dividing line with the Gnostics. Those sects couldn't abide the idea of God undergoing a physical incarnation, much less returning to a dead and entombed body. Why would you even need a doctrine like that if salvation came from mystical truths instead of the historical hill of Calvary? The answer is, you don't, and the Gnostics said it as often as they could.

The Original Story

How do you defend against a pseudo-Christianity that sounds attractive but gets the main thing wrong? When heretics came creeping into the ancient churches or lurked outside the doors to steal away the sheep—sounding so persuasive because they looked so much the same—the trick to recognize them was to ask, "Was this the original, apostolic preaching?" Irenaeus replied: "No way!" The storyline that the apostles proclaimed centered on the Lord Jesus Christ who was incarnated, crucified, risen, and returning soon for bodily resurrection and eternal judgment or reward. All that stuff about ghostly bodies and secret knowledge came much later and was therefore wrong.

To be a Christian doesn't just mean practicing a moral lifestyle, quoting from the Bible, and throwing around the name of Jesus as a respectable figure. Any Gnostic could do that. And people are still doing it today. World religions often make reference to Jesus or even hold him up as a divine figure. But upon closer inspection, they're found to be false. Beyond the religious cults, certain movements within evangelicalism like to attach Jesus or a Bible verse to their entirely non-Christian agendas. Sometimes these movements contain partial truths or are couched in churchy language. But is it really the gospel? You have to decide for yourself whether today's truth claims are from God himself or are heresy, plain and simple. And if you determine something is false, don't hold back in naming it as such. Because heresy is at its most dangerous when it seems most like the truth.

Such people are false apostles, deceitful workers,
masquerading as apostles of Christ ...
Their end will be what their actions deserve.

2 Corinthians 11:13,15

It's Okay to Be Catholic

There's a phrase in the popular statement of faith called the Apostles' Creed that makes many Protestants feel funny when they recite it: "I believe in the holy catholic church." Wait a minute! Didn't Protestants separate from the Roman Catholic Church and start something different? Why use this term? We will explore the use and development of creeds in a later chapter, so investigating the language of the Apostles' Creed isn't my goal at the moment. Instead, let's focus on that word *catholic* so we can see what it meant in the ancient church and why it became so common.

The Latin adjective *catholicus* came over from the Greek language. The etymology of the Greek term is based on two words: the preposition *kath-*, "pertaining to," and the noun *holos*, which means "whole." Thus, the Greek adjective *katholikos* (like its Latin form with a *c*) means "pertaining to the whole," that is, "general, universal, total."

You can see from this etymology that when the term *catholic* was applied to the Christian church, its primary and original purpose was to describe the church's universality and worldwide unity. Later, the term came to mean other things, such as doctrinal orthodoxy or communion with the bishop in Rome. But that was not its first meaning. In the days of the ancient church, the point of calling the church "catholic" wasn't to show that it was led by a pope in the Eternal City. Rather, the early church fathers were trying to say that all Christian congregations across the earth partake in a deep spiritual unity through Jesus Christ, their risen Lord and Head.

Orthodoxy and Heresy in Earliest Christianity

In the previous chapter, we encountered the teachings of Gnosticism. Various sects were usually named after the founder of their particular branch, each of which had its own doctrinal nuances, but all of which centered around the theme of salvation through knowledge. While any one of these sects was small, together they added up to quite a few people who thought of themselves as Christians. Yes, that's right. They believed they were the true Christians. They didn't perceive themselves as a cult, a sect, or a heresy. They claimed to be the true church of Jesus Christ, while the ignorant commoners who emphasized his bodily death and resurrection had gotten it all wrong.

But Gnosticism wasn't the only Christian competitor back then. Many other groups, now recognized as heresies, proliferated as well. The Ebionites were one of these. Although it's hard to trace the precise meaning of their name, we do know what they believed: A form of Jewish Christianity that taught works salvation by keeping the law of Moses. In other words, they were the descendants of the Judaizers whom Paul had criticized so vehemently in Galatians.

Another heresy was led by a rich businessman named Marcion. His view was the exact opposite of the Ebionites. Marcion and his followers believed that everything Jewish was bad. In fact, Yahweh himself was a harsh and contemptible god. He was a different deity than the loving Father of Jesus, who came to free us from Yahweh's incompetent reign. Therefore, the Marcionites threw out the Old Testament, and they excised from the New Testament anything that smacked of Judaism.

Beyond all these, many other pseudo-Christian sects proliferated as well. Often they held to extreme acts of bodily mortification, renouncing sexuality or even marriage itself (the Encratites). None of these groups worshiped the traditional gods of Rome. They all claimed to be the real version of Christianity, to have the true understanding of what Jesus was all about. I think you get the point. The ancient world abounded with competing views about Jesus, especially during the second century when these sects began to spread like wildfire. Who could say which one was right? If you decided you liked Jesus in those days, you had a bewildering array of options for how you might choose to reverence him.

Since one particular form of Christianity eventually triumphed— the right one, which centered on the risen Lord—it's often hard for us to recognize how vigorous and viable those other groups were. We tend to think they were universally recognized as false, like weird cults from the fringe. To use a canine analogy, historians have tended to tell the story of Christianity as if the mighty shepherd dog of Christianity came bounding onto the scene and defeated the malicious wolf of Rome. Although the little Chihuahuas of heresy nipped at the big dog's heels, it easily shook them off and went on its way. But it wasn't like that. It was actually one huge dog fight, with all the barking mongrels evenly matched. And the historian who first pointed this out was an important German scholar named Walter Bauer.

Readers of this book who study biblical Greek will know the name of Walter Bauer because he was the founding editor of the Greek dictionary that everyone uses today to study the New Testament. But Bauer was more than just a lexicologist. In 1934, he published a German book, translated into English in 1971, called *Orthodoxy and Heresy in Earliest Christianity.* This book articulated what has come to be called the Bauer Thesis. In a nutshell, Bauer argued that in many regions of the Roman Empire, the kind of Christianity that we practice today wasn't the first version there, nor was it the leading type when it finally did arrive. Quite often, the death-and-resurrection Christians were perceived to hold a newfangled view and were numerically small compared to other Jesus-religions that had gotten there first. These other kinds of "Christianity"—many of which didn't emphasize Jesus' resurrection at all—had a greater claim to being the original form of the faith in those particular regions.

So how did the resurrection group eventually win out across the Roman Empire? Bauer says that Rome achieved this domination through bribery and power politics. The Christian view at Rome—that Jesus died for humanity's sins and rose bodily from the grave—had no more claim to being true than any of its competitors. The Roman church just used name-calling and devious tactics to claim the mantle of "orthodoxy." Although Rome's view was no more right than any other, the Bauer Thesis suggests it managed to defeat the rest by branding them as latecomers and heretics. In this way, it finally won the battle and became the only type of Christianity. But that wasn't because of its inherent truth. Rome only won because of dirty tricks.

For a long time, Bauer's radical ideas rested quietly in the dusty libraries of German universities. But once the book came over into English, it fit perfectly with rising themes of academic postmodernism. Today it is taken for granted in the religion departments of American universities that what we call Christianity can't claim to be anything other than one particular view of Jesus out of many equally valid ones—the view that happened to win, to be sure, but not because it had any abiding truth value. Its victory was nothing but chance, while any of the others could have been just as good. You can see how this historical thesis fits perfectly with the postmodern idea that there is no such thing as absolute truth, just different personal truths vying for supremacy.

The One, Holy, Catholic, and Apostolic Church

Is the Bauer Thesis correct? Yes and no. On the one hand, there's no question that many different Jesus-religions proliferated in the second century, and even into the third, fourth, and fifth centuries before they were finally squelched. Some of these groups had roots in the first century—that is, in the age of the apostles. This is historically provable and should not be denied. Yet I believe the Bauer Thesis is incorrect in its fundamental argument that all versions of Christianity have equal claim to validity, and that a particular version won because of Rome's power.[1] No, the historical evidence shows that there was a single,

---

1. If you want to read more about these issues, see Paul Hartog, ed., *Orthodoxy and Heresy in Early Christian Contexts: Reconsidering the Bauer Thesis* (2015). I contributed a chapter in this book along with several other evangelical authors.

distinct version of Christianity at the very beginning: the version that proclaimed the risen Christ. It won not because it was sneaky, but because it was original and true.

Now of course, there was great diversity in the preaching of the early Christians. The widespread churches of the Roman Empire all had their own theological distinctives. But while the good news often had different shapes and nuances in various areas, at its heart, it was the same basic proclamation. It's like pizza. Despite regional variations, pizza is still pizza, whether in Italy, New York, Chicago, or the freezer of your local grocery store. Pizza isn't green beans. It isn't chicken soup. Those are other things, even though they're in the general category of food. Just as pizza stands alone as something identifiably unique (even if it exhibits variety here or there), the first form of Christianity that proclaimed Jesus' resurrection was unique. The Gnostics, Ebionites, Marcionites, and all the rest of the Jesus-religions were obviously something else. To pretend that they were just other kinds of "pizza" would be ridiculous. These were separate faiths, not other kinds of Christianity. Their fundamental elements were distinct.

Though my pizza analogy is (of course) modern, the argument I'm making here is an ancient one. It was made by the church fathers themselves. Their defense against heretics who claimed to be legitimate Christians appealed to the twin ideas of *apostolicity* and *catholicity*. Let me lay this out for you so you can understand the word *catholic* in its original context.

The first Christian writer to use the expression "catholic church" was Ignatius, bishop of Antioch, who died as a martyr around the year 115. His only surviving writings are the seven letters he wrote while he was being transported in chains from Antioch to Rome, where he would be thrown to the wild beasts in the Colosseum. One of his letters was written to the church at Smyrna. Ignatius knew that all kinds of shady teachers were plaguing the Smyrnaean church, so he gave the Christians there a word of pastoral counsel. He told them to consider the trustworthy bishop as the marker of the right community to associate with. Real bishops got their doctrines straight from the apostles themselves. Ignatius wrote, "All of you should follow the bishop like Jesus Christ follows the Father, and follow the elders like the apostles…Wherever the bishop shall appear, there let the congregation be; just as, wherever Jesus Christ is, there is the catholic church."[2]

Do you see Ignatius' point? Though he was the first to make it, many others followed after him (such as Irenaeus of Lyon and Tertullian of Carthage). The church of Jesus Christ had spread over a large area. But false pretenders had cropped up too, like the ones we've been discussing. So the two ancient lines of defense against the heretics' claims of legitimacy were apostolicity and catholicity. The church fathers insisted that the worldwide church proclaimed the foundational message of the apostles, and no other. The core content of the original gospel can be seen, for example, in Peter's preaching in Acts 2. The apostles taught that the crucified Christ is now the risen Lord.

As the decades moved on and the apostles passed the baton to the next generation, who retained Christianity's foundational message? It was the trustworthy bishops—supported by their godly elders and deacons—who preached nothing other than what was taught at the beginning. The universal church proclaims the original, apostolic message. By contrast, heresies can easily be identified as later aberrations so that no one will fall into their snares.

In the early church, the word *catholic* wasn't loaded with all the concepts we give it today. It was just a way of describing the universal, holistic, and widespread unity that all Christian congregations possessed because they adhered to the apostolic message. Unlike the pseudo-Christian sects that popped up here and there, creating independent conventicles wherever they went, the real church was unified, it was spiritual, it was worldwide, and it was rooted in the original gospel. That is why the Nicene Creed, which was formulated in the fourth century and is still recited today, used the fourfold expression, "We believe in one, holy, catholic, and apostolic church."[3] To be catholic is to be unified across a wide area by the true message of the Lord. So the

---

2. *Letter to the Smyrnaeans* 8.1, translation mine.

3. See chapter 14 for a discussion of the Apostles' Creed and the Nicene Creed.

next time someone asks whether you're a Protestant or a Catholic, you can reply with a confident smile, "I'm both."

> *Christ himself gave the apostles, the prophets, the*
> *evangelists, the pastors and teachers, to equip his people*
> *for works of service, so that the body of Christ may*
> *be built up until we all reach unity in the faith.*

EPHESIANS 4:11-13

◆ 5 ◆

The Spirits of the Dead Should Live in Your Church

I n my youth group culture of the 1980s, we used to have a thing called a "lock-in." At an appointed time, usually a Friday night after the high school football games, the teenagers of the church would bring their sleeping bags and assemble in the youth room for a big party. There would be games, a Bible talk from the youth pastor, and lots of pizza and soft drinks. And then, true to the event's name, the church doors would be locked and everyone spent the night on the floor.

Of course, a big part of the fun was sneaking around in the church after dark. It was exciting to be somewhere at night that you normally saw only by day. With no adults around, a quiet hush settled on the hallways and sanctuary. The moonlight streaming through the windows made the church seem like an entirely different place—a much more forbidding one. Some of the planned games lent themselves to this eerie feeling. There was one game where the kids played the role of early Christians being hunted by "Roman soldiers." And of course, these events also generated whispered tales of the ghosts that might be lurking around the corner, ready to snatch an unsuspecting teen. Is that what I mean by "The Spirits of the Dead Should Live in Your Church"?

Let the reader understand: This chapter is *not* about ghosts roaming the church's halls. All that is just kid stuff. It's not the point I'm making here at all. You might be thinking, *Well then, professor, what is your title above trying to say?* Let me lay it out for you. Once you understand my real claim, I think you'll begin to think in some new ways about the Christian faith, based on the insights of the ancient church.

The Communion of the Saints

In the previous chapter, we mentioned a phrase from the Apostles' Creed. Here's another one: "I believe...in the communion of the saints." It's one of those seemingly bland statements that you can say aloud without really thinking about what it means. Often we attach a rather superficial idea to it: that all Christians are friendly to one another, and we have fond affection in our hearts for our brothers and sisters in the Lord. But in its original context, this phrase—though it did include the idea of friendship—meant a whole lot more than first meets the eye.

The "communion" part of this phrase refers to the biblical concept of *koinōnia*, a deep and abiding fellowship that creates spiritual oneness. All believers in Jesus Christ are bound by this unity from the Holy Spirit. Though it is an inward unity, it is visualized in an outward way by the bread and cup that Christians share (see 1 Corinthians 10:16, which uses the word *koinōnia* to describe the Lord's Supper).

But what about the "saints"? That too is a biblical word: *hagioi*. In Scripture, it doesn't refer to super-spiritual people who stand above the rest. It just means all Christians. For example, Paul writes to Philemon and says, "I thank my God always when I remember you in my prayers, because I hear of your love and of the faith that you have toward the Lord Jesus and for all the saints" (Philemon 1:4-5 ESV). Yet there is also a narrower nuance of this word. Speaking about the great harlot of Babylon, the apostle John says, "I saw the woman, drunk with the blood of the saints, the blood of the martyrs of Jesus" (Revelation 17:6 ESV). Here, the saints are those who have shed their blood for Christ as martyrs.

In one sense, all Christians are *hagioi*, "holy ones." We have all been sanctified by Christ through repentance and faith. But in another sense, we recognize that some people attain a degree of spiritual maturity that most of us do not ever reach. Perhaps it is a godly grandmother, or a wise mentor, or someone with such a level of devotion that they stand out from the Christian crowd. In this secondary sense, a saint is a person who is rightly lifted up for everyone's admiration—and also, let us hope, for emulation. Saints are supposed to serve as good examples to the rest of us.

In the ancient church, the Christians knew they needed lots of motivation to persevere through the ostracism or persecution that would come their way. They did this by frequently setting holy examples before the community. Along with the temptation to deny one's faith, there was constant sexual temptation in the erotic culture of ancient Rome. Just about any waitress in a tavern would take the customer "upstairs" for a small fee. Brothels were always within a short walking distance of any urban house or apartment. Prostitutes could be visited for the price of a loaf of bread. And anyone who owned a slave could do whatever they wished with that person. In such a hypersexualized and morally decadent society, the early Christians made a special habit of setting forth exemplary lives so everyone knew what kind of virtues they should aspire to. These role models came to be called saints in the narrower sense of the word.

Now here's an important thing about saints: They don't stop being saintly when they die. In fact, their noble deaths often put a martyr's crown on their long and holy lives. The saints who have died in this world can still serve as moral examples—perhaps the best examples of all since their whole stories have been written and we know they finished well. The Bible tells us to be aware of our spiritual forefathers and foremothers who deserve special honor. The so-called Faith Hall of Fame in Hebrews 11 does exactly this. Then the next chapter urges Christians to be worthy of these heroic examples. Hebrews 12:1-2 says, "Therefore, since we are surrounded by such a great cloud of witnesses, let us throw off everything that hinders and the sin that so easily entangles. And let us run with perseverance the race marked out for us, fixing our eyes on Jesus, the pioneer and perfecter of faith."

The early church could celebrate the "cloud of witnesses" without worshiping them as deities because it didn't teach what the pagans did about the afterlife. The pagans believed that dead spirits became amorphous ghosts called "shades" who lived in the underworld, or who hovered around household shrines to bless the family with good luck. But Christians didn't worship their ancestors like the Romans did. Instead, they believed that dead souls belonged to Christ and would be raised up at the last trumpet to be with him forever. Until then, they slept in the ground, awaiting the second coming. And because these deceased Christians hadn't disappeared into nothingness, but were still "themselves" while they awaited resurrection, they could be celebrated in church as people worth emulating.

This, then, is what communion of the saints originally meant. It wasn't just friendly fellowship with living believers but spiritual kinship with dead ones too. Perhaps this sounds strange to you, even pagan. Certainly the Romans did practice a robust cult of the dead. But the early Christians were simply trying to live out what Paul had declared so boldly in 1 Thessalonians 4:13-14: "Brothers and sisters, we do not want you to be uninformed about those who sleep in death...For we believe that Jesus died and rose again, and so we believe that God will bring with Jesus those who have fallen asleep in him."

Deceased Christians aren't gone from us. No part of Christ's body is ever amputated and thrown away to rot. The dead are still part of the church while they wait for their Savior to return. We should by no means forget them. So powerful was this commemorative urge that the ancient Christians felt compelled to live it out not just in their churches through verbal tributes, but more tangibly, in the very place where the dead slept: the catacombs outside the city walls.

The Underground Church

Many believers today have heard of the catacombs, the burial grounds of the early Christians. During the first century AD, most Romans cremated their dead, and the Christians seem to have done likewise. But by the second century it become more common in ancient society to bury corpses in niches dug from the walls of underground tunnels. Then the niche would be sealed with a marble slab on which the deceased's name or a hopeful inscription could be carved. The Christians adopted this practice with gusto; for by preserving the body and recording some identifying information—often saying that such-and-such now rested "in peace"—the believers expressed their abiding hope in an individual afterlife with Jesus, who is "the firstfruits of those who have fallen asleep" (1 Corinthians 15:20).

The Christians even gave new names to such places. The pagans called them a *necropolis*, a city of the dead. But in addition to *catacombs*, which meant a dug-out place, the Christians also called it a *cemetery*, a place for sleeping. Why was the sleep metaphor so important? The thing about going to sleep is, you expect to eventually wake up. Unlike what the gods could offer, future bodily resurrection (literally, "standing up again") was promised to those who had died in Christ. That was good news indeed!

In-ground burial appealed to Christians because it pictured the theological truth of individual resurrection. So popular was this new practice that by the turn of the third century, the church's leaders were buying suburban land for exclusive Christian use.[1] Over the next few centuries, the church gradually excavated huge, multi-leveled mazes below the surface to meet the demand for all the people who wanted to be buried this way. Some wealthy Christians even reserved underground vaults for their whole household, often hiring artists to paint biblical scenes on the walls. These lovely frescos are the starting point in a long history of Christian art.

Today, a mythology has grown up around the catacombs. Legend would have us believe that the Christians lived there all the time, or at least that they went down every Sunday like little moles who shun daylight. Some people imagine that the Christians hid in the catacombs so the Romans couldn't arrest them and throw them to the lions. But none of this true. The catacombs weren't places to escape persecution. No one lived in the tunnels or came there on a weekly basis. These were

---

1. The Romans had strict laws that said no human body could ever be buried inside a city's walls. All burial grounds were located outside a city, usually near the gates so mourners could easily access them.

tombs, not cathedrals. They were dark and cold, and probably smelled like death no matter how well the graves were sealed. You didn't stay in such places for hours on end.

Nevertheless, small groups of Christians did visit the catacombs on a regular basis. After descending the staircase from the surface with flickering oil lamps in their hands, the believers would wind their way through tunnels to the wall niches where their relatives were buried. Or they might go to a famous martyr's grave instead. And then they would do something strange: The Christians would share a meal there, even pouring out a little wine for their loved one who was "sleeping." This wasn't exactly a Lord's Supper, for that was a different (though overlapping) ritual. Even so, by partaking of food in the presence of the grave, the Christians signaled that they still had *koinōnia* with the departed saint.

This ancient practice, though theologically reasonable in its original intent, was susceptible to getting off track. The common folk sometimes veered into superstition and started petitioning the dead saints for favors (which is what started the Roman Catholic practice of praying to saints). Or the banquets could get out of hand. After a little observance at the grave, the celebration back on the surface could turn into a raucous picnic with feasting, drinking, and dancing. Sometimes the bishops had to admonish their people not to let the holy remembrance of revered Christians turn into an excuse for partying in the countryside.

But after setting these inaccurate practices aside, we are left with the core idea of actively celebrating the lives of deceased saints. This is based on the solid doctrinal foundation of bodily resurrection and the preservation of each person's identity after death. For Christians, the dead really do need to be alive, so to speak, in our midst. We're not talking here about spirits haunting the sanctuary or knocking books off the shelves of the church library. Creepy ghost stories like that are just nonsense. Instead, if we learn from the wisdom of the ancients, we will find creative ways to make sure that those who ran the race before us aren't forgotten. Today's churches should strive to put these holy examples before our eyes—both the notable heroes of church history and the less famous ones who made your local church what it is. If you can find a way to do this well, you will discover that the "communion of the saints" is a whole lot richer than you first imagined.

> *Do not marvel at this, for an hour is coming when all who are in the tombs will hear his voice and come out, those who have done good to the resurrection of life, and those who have done evil to the resurrection of judgment.*

JOHN 5:28-29 ESV

6

There's No Way Around It: Christianity Is for Misfits

I f there's one thing the ancient church can teach us, it's how to live as a misfit. An outsider. A pilgrim in a foreign land. Americans definitely aren't used to that because we're accustomed to living in a Christianized society. Perhaps it's less visible today than it used to be, but a Christian worldview is still very much in place beneath the surface of the United States. The structuring principles of our society come from the Judeo-Christian tradition. Although public assumptions about religion have certainly changed in the past decades, the edifice of American life still stands upon a Christian foundation.

But nothing lasts forever. A culture will change its fundamental values as the wheel of history turns. The day will come—if it hasn't arrived already—when Christianity will be considered an irrelevant superstition that everyone can safely ignore. People will view the church as incomprehensible at best and detrimental at worst. The number of committed Christians will dwindle to a tiny minority in our society. Europe and Canada have already moved in this direction. When this view permeates the United States, will Americans know how to live?

The early Christians can teach us a lot about being cultural outsiders. For three hundred years, it never even crossed their minds that things could be otherwise. Even when the tide began to turn under

Emperor Constantine (which is a story for a different chapter), the Christians still understood that they had to forge a different kind of society than the one they had inherited. A Christian must always be resolutely countercultural. It is essential to our faith to be different from the world. Like it or not, if we're doing Christianity right, we're going to be cultural misfits.

Pagan Rome

What kind of society was Christianity born into? It's worth taking a look at Jesus' own experience, and the apostles' after him, and the generations' after that. At no point in the first three centuries of church history was Roman society a welcoming place for the new faith.

Let's start at the beginning. Luke 2:1 tells us, "In those days Caesar Augustus issued a decree that a census should be taken of the entire Roman world." It was this census that prompted Joseph to take his wife Mary to Bethlehem, where, as we all know, Jesus was born. Who was this powerful fellow called Caesar Augustus, the man who could issue commands to the whole world?

The short answer is, he was the first Roman emperor—but his city had been around a long time before him. Ancient Rome was founded when several hilltop villages merged to form a single city. This happened eight centuries before Christ, around the same time that the prophet Isaiah was active in Israel. At first, the new city of Rome was ruled by kings. When they became too powerful, the Romans rejected monarchy and transformed themselves into a republic run by a large, voting senate. For five hundred years before Christ, the Roman Republic expanded its territory by conquering more and more people.

But then civil war broke out. When Rome's most powerful leader, Julius Caesar, was assassinated in 44 BC, his nephew and adopted son, Octavian, took over. Octavian defeated all his enemies and was the last man standing. Now he even had control of the senate. Octavian wasn't just a powerful senator or military general. He was essentially a king again. But he couldn't call himself that. So in 27 BC, he renamed himself Caesar Augustus and took the title of emperor. In this way, the

Roman Empire was born just as the true Lord of lords was about to come into the world.

Although Jesus wasn't a political revolutionary, his kingdom definitely stood opposed to Rome. Many Jews in those days wanted the radical new teacher from Nazareth to do more than preach. They wanted him take up the sword and fight against the imperial overlords they hated so much. This wasn't, of course, what Jesus had come to do. Yet that didn't mean he hadn't come to overthrow Rome.

The clash of power between the kingdom of God and the earthly kingdom is a major theme that runs right through the New Testament. We see it in the first Gospel when Jesus tells Pilate that he is, in fact, the true king of the Jews (Matthew 27:11). And we see it in Revelation 17 when the harlot of Babylon is seated upon a beast with seven heads, representing a city built on seven hills—a clear reference to Rome. In the book of Acts, Paul faces various Roman officials and eventually goes to the capital city to confront the wicked Nero. The gospel is the only force that can defeat Rome's wealth and power.

Now let us be clear: There is no hint of insurrection or revolution in the Bible. The early Christians obeyed the laws and prayed for their emperors (Matthew 22:21; Romans 13:1; 1 Timothy 2:2; 1 Peter 2:13-17). Even so, they believed that Jesus, not Caesar, would be proven the true Lord of the world (Romans 10:9; Philippians 2:9-11; Revelation 19:11-16).

Why was the Roman Empire so diametrically opposed to God? What kind of people were in charge of it? In chapter 4, we discussed some ancient religions like Gnosticism that were hostile to the Christian church. But in the enormous sweep of the empire, the Gnostics and other heresies added up to a very small number. The people who controlled the government, the army, and all the structures of society weren't members of these heretical sects. They were the pagans who worshiped the ancient gods of Rome. And all the commoners went right along with them, for they were just as devoted to the gods as the people at the top. This was a society that prided itself on having more religious devotion than anyone else. As the great Roman statesman Cicero bragged, "It is by means of piety and religion, and the special wisdom of perceiving that all things are governed by the divine power of the immortal gods, that we are superior to all other countries and nations."[1]

Modern Americans aren't used to thinking of the government as something religious. Ever since the days of Thomas Jefferson, there has been a "wall of separation between Church and State."[2] Sure, there are individuals who practice various religions, and some of these folks are involved in politics or work in the civic bureaucracy. But their faith is expected to be a private affair. Neither the federal government in Washington nor the state houses in our capitals nor the city halls of our local mayors are religious institutions. They're supposed to be spiritually neutral. America is a thoroughly secular nation, and more so every day.

Nothing could be further from the experience of the early Christians. To look for a modern parallel to their situation, we would have to think of a fiercely committed theocracy like Iran, Saudi Arabia, or Afghanistan. Or we might look at North Korea, which requires devotion to the supreme leader just as in ancient Rome. Worshiping the pagan gods wasn't something you could choose to do on the side. There was no secular living for six days and a day of piety on the seventh. Every aspect of Roman life—its politics, military, courts, literature, commerce, agriculture, education, bath houses, theaters, sports—was intertwined with the divine pantheon. And this was why the early Christians didn't expect their alternate form of religion to be well received by their society. The Romans had been committed to paganism for as long as anyone could remember. Christians were going to be misfits in that society, no matter what. Their crucified Messiah made certain of that.

Speaking the Culture's Language

Despite their misfit status, the Christians didn't withdraw into enclaves that no one could penetrate. Sure, they kept a degree of secrecy in their churches for the sake of safety, but the Great Commission

---

1. *Response to the Soothsayers* 19. Throughout this book, I have sometimes adapted the quotations slightly for clarity to modern readers.

2. Jefferson's "Letter to the Danbury Baptists" can be read at the U.S. Library of Congress website here: https://www.loc.gov/loc/lcib/9806/danpre.html.

demanded that they also reach out. They did so with gusto. And they didn't just do it in one-on-one conversations. In the second and third centuries, a new generation of intellectuals rose up to defend the true faith to the pagan world. Church history refers to them as the apologists, a name which comes from the Greek word for a speech of self-defense. These apologists weren't slaves or simple folk of the lower classes, but scholars trained in Greco-Roman philosophy and rhetoric. They took it upon themselves to put the Christian faith into words that the pagan culture could comprehend. Even if most of the unbelievers didn't convert, at least they might view Christianity with more sympathy. That, in itself, would be a victory.

One of the foremost Christian apologists of the time was a man named Justin, from the region of Samaria, near the place where Jesus had met the woman at the well (John 4:1-41). Justin was an expert in the Greek philosophy of his day. He especially favored the doctrines of Plato. In the second century AD, many people had a Platonic worldview. Not everyone knew that their ideas went back to this famous Greek philosopher, who had been dead for 500 years, but it was true. The same thing often happens today. Many of our popular beliefs have philosophical underpinnings that originally arose in universities and spread into the wider culture. Justin knew the intellectual ideas that bubbled beneath the surface of his society, so he reformulated Christianity in a way that would be easier for people to understand.

In particular, Justin emphasized the Platonic idea of a spiritual world above and a physical world below. How are those two worlds bridged? Some Platonist philosophers had proposed a divine entity called the *logos*. This Greek word referred to the "logical" principle in the cosmos. Another translation of *logos* was "word." The *logos* could mediate truth from the world above to the world below, just as a verbal word is spoken from an immaterial mind into a physical ear.

But here's where things get interesting. *Logos* was also the term the apostle John used when he wrote in his Gospel, "In the beginning was the *logos*, and the *logos* was with God, and the *logos* was God...And the *logos* became flesh and dwelt among us" (John 1:1,14). Justin realized that this was how he could contextualize the Bible's message to a

Platonic world. He essentially told whomever would listen, "You are right to believe in the *logos*, but you're missing the rest of the story! What you don't know is that the *logos* became flesh. His name is Jesus Christ, and only he can lead you from the physical world down here to the heavenly world above." This was a message that made sense to many people. They converted to God because of the work of apologists like Justin.

Unfortunately, Justin's bold apologetics got him in trouble with local officials after he moved to Rome. Enemies trumped up charges against him, and soon he was facing the death penalty. Because he would not deny his Savior, this great apologist is known in history as Justin Martyr, having paid the ultimate price for his faith.

Prepared to Give an Answer

The text that recorded Justin Martyr's trial and death has come down to us today. In it, we clearly see the opposition between pagan society and Christianity. Justin was hauled before the mayor of Rome, a man named Rusticus. It happened like this:

> Turning to Justin, the mayor said, "Are you convinced that if I have you whipped and beheaded you'll go up to heaven?"
>
> "If I endure these things, then yes, I have hope because of my endurance," Justin replied. "I know God's blessing will remain upon everyone who lives a devout life, lasting even through the final judgment by fire."
>
> "So you suppose you'll ascend to heaven?"
>
> "I don't just suppose it. I'm absolutely certain of it."
>
> "If you don't obey me," Mayor Rusticus said, "you will be punished."
>
> But Justin replied, "If we are punished, we have the sure promise of salvation."

Mayor Rusticus then proclaimed, "Let those who refused to sacrifice to the gods be whipped and led away for execution in accordance with the laws."[3]

This historical event illustrates what we mentioned at the outset of this chapter: The implacable opposition between Rome and the followers of Jesus. The early Christians like Justin were willing to stand for the Lord without compromise, no matter what kind of scorn—or worse—their culture might heap on them. How could they do this so boldly? Because they had already reconciled themselves to their misfit status. They didn't expect to be accepted, celebrated, or embraced. The only compliment they wanted to hear was Jesus' words, "Well done, good and faithful servant…Enter into the joy of your master" (Matthew 25:21 ESV). May that affirmation be enough for us as well.

Even if you should suffer for what is right, you are blessed.
"Do not fear their threats; do not be frightened." But in your hearts
revere Christ as Lord. Always be prepared to give an answer to
everyone who asks you to give the reason for the hope that you have.

1 PETER 3:14-15

---

3. Litfin, *Martyr Stories*, 69.

7

Your Pastor Deserves to Be Put on a Pedestal

One of the most important documents in American life is the Declaration of Independence. Its second sentence expresses a foundational principle of our country: "We hold these truths to be self-evident, that all men are created equal, that they are endowed by their Creator with certain unalienable Rights, that among these are Life, Liberty and the pursuit of Happiness."

The notion that all people are created equal hasn't been the predominant view in human history. Most societies have assumed that people of the higher classes are intrinsically better than the lowly folk, having more rights and privileges than mere commoners. But not in the United States. Americans now hold to the egalitarian principle that every human being has the same value from the Creator. Therefore, no single individual is better than any other.

However, this view is wrong. Your pastor is, in fact, superior to you. Both the Bible and the church fathers say so. Surprising, but true.

Of course I'm not suggesting that your pastor is superior in the sense of being taller, faster, stronger, smarter, richer, or better looking. Some of those things might be true. Probably not richer, but maybe a few of the others. Yet none of them is what I'm talking about here.

Nor is your pastor worth more to God than you. He doesn't have more of the indwelling Holy Spirit than the people in the pews. His private life isn't necessarily more pure than yours. His thoughts aren't automatically wiser because he has been to seminary, or knows Greek and Hebrew, or has a doctorate, or has a sign on his door that says Pastor. Again, some of those things might be true. Yet it's not what I'm talking about here.

I'm referring to *honor*. By virtue of the pastoral vocation that has come to him from God, and the office that he occupies as a shepherd of souls, the person who pastors your church has a claim to superiority. Of course, he shouldn't lord it over you. Just the opposite: you should accord it to him without him needing to say a word. And you should do this even if you know that in certain ways, he's weak, fallible, and sinful. Assuming you aren't dealing with gross immorality or spiritual abuse, but just the regular shortcomings that everyone has, your pastor's foibles should be set aside with gracious disregard. You should put him on a pedestal, honor him with special names, and celebrate him to the rest of the congregation.

Why? Because the Bible says so. And afterward, the church fathers found it to be a wise idea as well. I suggest it's still wise today.

Double Honor

Let's consider the biblical view of spiritual leaders. To do this properly would require an entire book, so we will just look at the key points.

In the Old Testament, the Levites were the priests. Who were they? Remember that Jacob had 12 sons who founded Israel's 12 tribes. One of his sons, Levi, was special—not because the man himself was intrinsically better, but because God declared it to be so.

The descendants of Levi were commanded to serve as Israel's priests. In Numbers 3 we learn that these people had a special status. Normally, the firstborn son of a family was consecrated to God. This gave him unique rights and privileges. But in ancient Israel the Levites took the place of the firstborn. God declared to Moses, "I have taken the Levites from among the Israelites in place of the first male offspring of every Israelite woman. The Levites are mine, for all the firstborn are mine"

(Numbers 3:12-13). God also said that the Levites should receive a special portion from the other tribes, namely, one tenth of the Israel's harvest and livestock (Leviticus 27:30-33; Numbers 18:21). This was their due because they served as priests.

But wait, you might be thinking. *The Levites were priests. They deserved special honor in those days. But New Testament pastors aren't priests. They're just ordinary human beings. Shouldn't we have different rules today?* Fair enough. Modern pastors aren't intermediaries between God and humans. They don't bring animal sacrifices to a temple, or carry confessions and forgiveness back and forth. Even so, the Bible tells us they deserve special honor, just like the Levites of old.

In 1 Timothy 5:17-18, we read, "The elders who direct the affairs of the church well are worthy of double honor, especially those whose work is preaching and teaching. For Scripture says, 'Do not muzzle an ox while it is treading out the grain,' and 'The worker deserves his wages.'" Paul's phrase "double honor" is interesting. The apostle is talking here not just about giving respect, but backing up that respect with financial remuneration. That is his point about letting oxen feed, which is a Jewish law found in Deuteronomy 25:4. A beast that works hard should partake of the fruit of its labors. Paul also quotes the words of Jesus in Luke 10:7, where the Lord says that anyone who works deserves to be paid. When it comes to pastors, Paul declares that their work deserves double pay. These men teach and preach in the church—a calling that causes them to be judged by God more strictly than people in the congregation (James 3:1).

Bishops, Presbyters, and Deacons

When Paul speaks about pastors in the passage above, what Greek word does he use? It is *presbyteros,* one of the three main words for pastoral offices in the early church. Usually translated as "elders," this word refers to men who have lived long enough to have a track record of godliness that earns the respect of the church.

A second word is *overseer,* or in Greek, *episkopos.* The prefix *epi-* means "over," and perhaps you can discern the word *scope* in the second part. An *episkopos* is someone who has "scope over" something, that is, he has oversight. This is why the word is usually translated in the New Testament as overseer. But through the centuries of church history, the sound of the word also morphed through late Latin *ebiscopus* and Middle English *bischop* to become our modern word, *bishop*.

The third biblical word for an office in the church is *diakonos*. This term refers to a servant or minister, someone who carries out practical tasks for the church. In Acts 6:1-6, seven men are chosen to "serve tables." The word "serve" is a verb form of *diakonos*. Later, in the Pastoral Epistles, the apostle Paul gives instructions to "elders" and then to "deacons."

In the Bible, a sharp distinction isn't made between presbyters and overseers. Both terms describe men who function as elders with doctrinal oversight and leadership responsibilities. This group is assisted in practical matters by the deacons. All these men, as well as female deaconesses, were supposed to have exceptionally high moral character. They cooperated in harmony. But was it leadership by committee? Did no one ever take charge of the group?

The Monepiscopacy

It's true that early Christian house churches were led by multiple men, assisted in various tasks by godly women. (We will discuss the roles of women in the ancient church in the next chapter.) Although leadership was a group affair, certain men did stand out in various churches. The apostle James, for example, was prominent in Jerusalem. Peter led the church in Antioch, then later in Rome. On the island of Crete, Titus had special authority. While these were unofficial leadership roles, they were recognized by everyone. Often in human communities, respected figures rise up and take charge. It can be a very effective way of managing a group.

After the New Testament period ended, the Gnostics and other pseudo-Christian heresies began to multiply. By the beginning of the second century, it had become necessary to figure out which churches were truly apostolic and which were fakes. Ignatius of Antioch, whom we met in chapter 4, came up with a clever solution. It worked so well that other churches soon followed his lead.

Ignatius said that one main leader in each church should be the flag bearer around whom other Christians should rally. The true believers would distinguish themselves from heretics by staying close to a trustworthy figure. The real church in every city could be recognized by its leader who stood in the train of the apostles. This man would hold the same doctrine the first generation did, not the newfangled ideas of recently arrived heretics.

In order to give this single leader a recognizable name, Ignatius used the biblical word *episkopos* to identify him. He was the "overseer" of the congregation—the figure today whom we might call the "senior pastor." He was assisted in doctrinal matters by his council of elders (the presbyters), and in practical duties by his male and female deacons. This system eventually included other offices as well, such as readers, singers, doorkeepers, exorcists, and devoted virgins and widows. In this way, the ancient Christians adopted a hierarchical structure for their churches. Historians call this arrangement the *monepiscopacy*, meaning "one bishop" per city. Of course, the bishop wasn't an all-powerful tyrant, just the primary leader of a group of dedicated men and women.

Clergy and Laity

Bishops were held in high honor in the ancient church, along with presbyters and deacons too. This was partly because whenever persecutions broke out, the authorities typically targeted the leaders. To be a pastor in the ancient church often meant being a martyr. The Christians also respected these leaders because the Scriptures instructed them to, as we have already seen. In a culture that didn't have American equality as the mental framework but was quite used to honoring a certain class of people, it was natural to give reverence to bishops, elders, and deacons.

These pastoral offices were viewed as being parallel to the ancient priesthood of Israel. The epitaph on one Christian woman's grave says, "I, Petronia, wife of a Levite, of modest countenance, here lay down my bones in their resting place. Cease from weeping, my husband and sweet children, and believe that it is not right to mourn one that lives in God."[1] Petronia was the wife of a deacon, so she used an Old Testament term to designate him as a "Levite." She encouraged her husband and children not to mourn for her since she was now alive with God. We know nothing else about this fearless woman. Yet the brief words inscribed on her gravestone offer us a fascinating window into the ancient Christian mentality—not just about death, but about deacons.

Over time, the ancient church came to revere its pastors so much that they were set within a specific "order." This was a common Roman term for a grouping of people within society. We still use this term today when we speak of someone being "ordained" to ministry. Ordination gives a pastor special standing, not only within the church but even under secular tax law. In the ancient era, the primary sign of ordination was laying hands on the person (Acts 6:6; 1 Timothy 4:14). The order of the clergy was contrasted with the "laity," a word that referred to the general people within a congregation.

In the first few centuries of church history, the clergy weren't viewed as having any special powers. But gradually, around the beginning of the Middle Ages, the idea began to emerge that priests had unique sacramental powers due to their ordination. There was no specific moment when the original idea of a pastor worshipfully leading you into the presence of Christ, or respectfully presiding over the Lord's Supper, turned into the Roman Catholic concept of a priest who has powers to consecrate the elements of the Mass and mediate forgiveness of sins. The earlier idea, which was good and natural, gradually evolved into the later one.

Once it was established, it stuck around for many centuries. By the time of the Reformation in the 1500s, the Catholic concept of the priesthood was due for a major correction. But all those debates in the sixteenth century were foreign to the early Christians. The first generations of church history just wanted to follow the Bible's lead when it came to honoring spiritual leaders. The bishops, presbyters, and

---

1. Henry Bettenson and Chris Maunder, *Documents of the Christian Church* (2011) 91.

deacons who were marked out by ordination had a special, God-given task. Because they guided and instructed eternal souls, their judgment was more strict. That was why, when they were faithful in their duties, their double honor was well deserved.

Is your own pastor worthy of such high regard? Even if the sermon last Sunday was boring or recent decisions weren't to your liking—yes, even so, this faithful laborer in the Lord's vineyard deserves your honor. The same is true of your elders, deacons, and deaconesses. These workers have been appointed to a sacred task. They deserve to be put on a high pedestal. For while it's true that "all men are created equal," not everyone is called to shepherd the flock of God.

Now we ask you, brothers and sisters, to acknowledge
those who work hard among you, who care for you
in the Lord and who admonish you. Hold them in
the highest regard in love because of their work.

1 THESSALONIANS 5:12-13

8

Christianity Created History's First Feminists

The word *feminist* is loaded with various connotations. Some readers will think of it as a hopeful and positive word. It describes people such as the Suffragettes of the early twentieth century who fought for women's right to vote. Or it celebrates brave and pioneering women like Florence Nightingale, Amelia Earhart, and Rosa Parks. In this context, feminism is a good thing because it defends the female gender from male abuse.

But there are negative images of feminism as well. Since many draw from stereotypes, I won't dredge them up here. Yet we have to admit that some kinds of feminism are troubling. People who have called themselves feminists have advocated neopagan ideas in which a supreme goddess is worshiped instead of the true God. In no way does the Bible support this kind of feminism. It condemns goddess worship as evil (e.g., Judges 3:7).

Although the ancient Christians rejected the female deities in the religions around them, they nevertheless celebrated the female gender. In this chapter, I would like to bust the myth that the Christian faith is domineering and oppressive to women. Admittedly, the structures and teachings of the church have been used to foster oppression through the centuries. But this is a sinful corruption of Christianity, not something that flows naturally from it. The truth is, there was no force in Greco-Roman society more liberating for women than the early church. It is no exaggeration to say that Christianity created the world's first feminists. Women found dignity and opportunity in the church that their pagan society never offered them.

The Feminine Ideal

To understand the Christian view of women, we must first understand how they were treated in the culture of ancient Rome. This society was patriarchal, a term which means "father-ruled." The head of a Roman household had the power of life or death over his entire family, though in practice it was rarely used. Yet the father was still the owner of his wife and children. Baby girls were usually given a female form of the father's name. Even after a daughter was married, she was still owned by her father unless her ownership was transferred to the new husband.

Women in Roman society could not vote or be elected to political office. They had to be under a man's control—father, husband, or pimp. The job of a typical woman was to honor the gods, marry a husband while in her teens, tend the home, and bear children. One ancient gynecologist said of his patients: "[W]omen are married for the sake of bearing children and heirs."[1] Or listen to this summary of a woman's life from her gravestone: "Here I lie, a matron named Veturia. My father was Veturius. My husband was Fortunatus. I lived for twenty-seven years, and I was married 16 years to the same man. After I gave birth to six children, only one of whom is still alive, I died."[2] Young Veturia died at age 27 after bearing six children for her man, losing all but one of them. As for her age at her wedding, you can do the math yourself.

Women in Early Christianity

The Roman background sets the stage for the coming of Christianity onto the scene. The new faith's revaluing of women began with Jesus himself. People don't always recognize this about Jesus, but his

---

1. Soranus of Ephesus, *Gynecology* 1.34.1, translated in Jo-Ann Shelton, *As the Romans Did: A Sourcebook in Roman Social History* (1988) 24.

2. Shelton, 292.

interaction with women was scandalous in his day. He had women disciples who followed him around, a major no-no in a time when women were supposed to be anchored to the home. In Luke's Gospel we learn that "Jesus traveled about from one town and village to another, proclaiming the good news of the kingdom of God. The Twelve were with him, and also some women who had been cured of evil spirits and diseases: Mary (called Magdalene) from whom seven demons had come out; Joanna the wife of Chuza, the manager of Herod's household; Susanna; and many others. These women were helping to support them out of their own means" (8:1-3).

The two most important jobs in human history were both assigned to women. The first was an act of childbearing. I don't just mean mothers giving birth in general, but Mary's specific task of bearing the Son of God. "Do not be afraid, Mary; you have found favor with God," said the angel to that timid virgin from Nazareth (Luke 1:30). And after this, who was the first person that God asked to proclaim Christ's resurrection as eyewitness testimony? Not one of the 12 disciples, nor any great ruler or king. It was a woman. Mary Magdalene was the first person ever to behold the risen Lord. He commissioned Mary, his devoted female disciple, to begin spreading the good news by declaring what she had seen (John 20:17-18). If this isn't a ringing endorsement of the feminine gender in God's plan, I don't know what is!

As the early church began to spread around the empire, women flocked to it. Clearly, Christianity wasn't viewed as "oppressive" like so many people say today. It required great personal sacrifice to become a Christian; so if it were oppressive, why would so many women convert? The fact is, women found the new faith liberating. Their culture treated them as second-class citizens who played an inferior role to the men who ran the government and fought in the army. Spousal abuse was rampant, and female slaves were sex objects for their masters.

But within the church, a different ethic prevailed. Christian husbands were taught to be gentle and self-sacrificing with their wives. Christian slave owners had to treat their servants with respect. Many women in ancient society found this to be a much better alternative to the world they knew. In fact, more women converted than men. One social scientist who has studied this topic declares, "Amidst contemporary denunciations of Christianity as patriarchal and sexist, it is easily forgotten that the early church was so especially attractive to women." Why was this the case? "Christianity was unusually appealing because within the Christian subculture women enjoyed far higher status than did women in the Greco-Roman world at large."[3]

This is not to say, of course, that the early Christians adopted twenty-first century views about women. There was no way for the ancients to step out of their value system and adopt ours. Women did not suddenly become masters of large businesses like today's female CEOs. Wars were never fought by female soldiers. Women weren't invited into the political arena as voting members of a fully democratic society. That didn't happen in ancient Rome, nor even in America until 1920. Christianity continued to follow these ancient cultural perspectives.

Some of the church fathers could be quite prudish in their remarks about women. For example, Tertullian informed women that "You are each an Eve...you are the devil's gateway,"[4] as if sin naturally accompanied their bodies at all times. Although Tertullian wrote many positive things about women, including a loving tribute to his wife, here he dipped into hyperbole (as he often did) in his desire to warn Christians about sexual temptation. It is unfortunate that Tertullian interpreted the story of Eve in such an insulting way.

Did the early Christians allow women to be pastors? Although various Gnostic sects often had women leaders, the orthodox church did not accept this practice. They heeded the biblical injunctions against it (e.g., 1 Timothy 2:12), so they considered the role of elders to be reserved for men. It is a strange aspect of contemporary church life that male eldership is viewed as oppressive to women. Is this necessarily true? The ancient Christians didn't think so because they didn't view pastoring as being about power. That is a carnal way of framing the issue: Who gets to make decisions? Who has the most prominent

---

3. Rodney Stark, *The Rise of Christianity* (1997) 95.

4. *On the Apparel of Women* 1.1.

and visible roles? Who is most highly paid? These considerations are the exact opposite of what pastoral ministry is actually about. Jesus said, "The greatest among you will be your servant" (Matthew 23:11).

When male elders function as servant leaders who sacrifice themselves for the flock, and when women in the church also lead in ways that are equally valuable in God's eyes, the whole church is harmonious. Neither gender grasps for power or position. Everyone seeks to give of themselves without a desire for recognition or acclaim. When Christians live like this, praise comes to them naturally, just as it should. Their lives please the Lord, and others see it and want to celebrate it. Early Christian women did not have to be pastors to be considered praiseworthy. The ancient church honored its heroines in other ways.

Great Christian Heroines

Even though women didn't normally function as elders or public teachers, we have every reason to believe they held important leadership positions in the local churches. We get a window into everyday Christian practice through the pictures painted on the walls of the catacombs. There we discover that women played an integral role in church life. They served the bread and wine of the communal meals, prayed in a standing posture, and sat alongside the men in worship. As my friend Lynn Cohick concludes, "In the echoes left in these ancient underground chambers, we can discern the voices of women who were active participants in Christian rituals and practices."[5]

Women weren't expected to stay silent whenever theology was under discussion at church. The early Christians had deep female thinkers in their midst. In the fourth century, we meet the famous theologian Macrina the Younger. Highly educated and exceptionally wise, this woman was celebrated by her brother, Gregory of Nyssa, as a theological dialogue partner who possessed great insight. Augustine's pious mother, Monica, discoursed with him in a similar fashion. And the brilliant linguistic scholar Jerome often had learned discussions

---

5. Lynn H. Cohick and Amy Brown Hughes, *Christian Women in the Patristic World* (2017) 86.

with his female friends, Paula and Marcella, both of whom were noted for their intellects. Clearly, theological study wasn't—and still isn't—a man's exclusive domain!

Women were also gloriously celebrated when they died as martyrs. One of the greatest heroines in all of church history was Perpetua of Carthage, whom we met in chapter 2. She was a young mother in her early twenties when a terrible persecution broke out. Instead of denying her faith, Perpetua stood strong for the Lord. While imprisoned in a harsh dungeon, she became an exemplary leader of her brothers and sisters, including her teacher Saturus. Perpetua's spiritual wisdom was highly revered by her fellow martyrs.

In the final days before Perpetua was cast into the amphitheater to be attacked by wild beasts, she wrote a diary about her experiences which was preserved by the local church at Carthage. An unknown Christian writer (quite possibly the supposed misogynist Tertullian) put an editorial framework around the diary and published it as a book. Here is how he described the noble martyr as she marched to her death: "Perpetua went along at a calm pace with a radiant countenance. She was a true wife of Christ, beloved of God. The intense expression in her eyes made all the onlookers avert their gaze."[6] The ancient church knew how to honor its heroines.

Early Christianity also offered ancient women one of the first viable lifestyles other than marriage and childbearing. Women could pledge themselves to celibacy (either from the virginity of their youth, or after becoming widows) and serve the church full-time for the rest of their lives. The beginnings of this practice are found in Scripture when a list of widows was maintained (Acts 6:1; 1 Timothy 5:9). These women were fed and clothed by the church, and in return they performed valuable ministry. The apostle Paul respects such a high calling when he says, "An unmarried woman or virgin is concerned about the Lord's affairs: Her aim is to be devoted to the Lord in both body and spirit" (1 Corinthians 7:34; see also v. 28).

The lives of these devoted women would be spent in worship, prayer,

---

6. Litfin, *Martyr Stories*, 104.

communal sisterhood, and service to the poor and needy. This was a very popular occupation for Christian women. One report tells us that in third-century Rome, in addition to the bishop, there were 46 presbyters, 7 deacons, 52 exorcists, readers, and doorkeepers...and more than 1,500 enrolled widows![7] Throughout church history, the gifts of these consecrated virgins (eventually called nuns) have resulted in great spiritual awakenings and immeasurable service to human society.

So the next time someone tells you that Christianity has always been oppressive to women, don't believe it. Oppression comes from sinners of all religions—including Christianity, unfortunately. Yet faith in Jesus is never oppressive. His imitators never denigrate people made in the image of God. History shows us that in the ancient world, if you were a feminist with a burning desire to reach your highest potential, you rejected Venus or Isis. Instead you became a follower of the true liberator, the Lord Jesus Christ.

> *There is neither Jew nor Gentile, neither slave nor free, nor is there male and female, for you are all one in Christ Jesus.*
>
> GALATIANS 3:28

---

7. Eusebius, *Church History* 6.43.11

9

Sexual Abstinence Is a Good Idea for Christians— Yes, Including You

We live in a sex-obsessed culture. Unfortunately, it only seems to be getting worse. Practices that once were taboo are now mainstream. Behaviors that once were private are now public. Deviances that once were shameful are now flaunted, even celebrated. Today, anybody can find the worst sort of debauchery with an easy click or a swipe. We live in a society saturated with explicit sexual messages and raw lust.

Although we tend to think of distant historical ages as having more conservative sexual values than today, in reality, ancient Rome was just as sex-saturated as our present world. While the ancients didn't have mass media to spread pornography, they did have the institution of slavery. The fact that slaves had no rights to their own bodies made sexual encounters cheap and readily available. Whether it was a slave owned by a lecherous master or one working as a prostitute for a pimp, a hookup was available to just about anyone. Modern visitors to the ancient ruins of Pompeii quickly learn this when they encounter street corner brothels with lurid paintings still visible on the walls. The price for a sexual encounter could be as cheap as two copper pennies, the same price as a loaf of bread. Obviously, the ancient Christians lived in a society just as decadent as ours—if not worse.

Like the Jews before them, the Christians had a radically different view of sexuality than their pagan counterparts. God had made his rules clear in the Law of Moses. The seventh commandment clearly states, "Thou shalt not commit adultery" (Exodus 20:14). This commandment was grounded, of course, in the teaching of Genesis 2:18-24 that men and women are intended to form permanent marriage bonds so that the two would become "one flesh" (v. 24).

When the early church emerged in the context of first-century Judaism, it inherited these Jewish sexual ethics. Jesus' own teaching established the marriage mandate in the garden of Eden as the divine norm (Matthew 19:3-12). The ancient Christians were thoroughly committed to sexual chastity. But what exactly did this look like? And did the ancient believers have any surprising views that might instruct us today?

Sex and the Single Girl...and Guy

In 1962, Helen Gurley Brown, the long-time editor of *Cosmopolitan* magazine, published a book called *Sex and the Single Girl* that was quickly turned into a movie. As a leader of the sexual revolution of the 1960s, Brown was an advocate for women's total autonomy, including their prerogative to have free sex as often as they wished. She is widely associated with the saying, "Good girls go to heaven; bad girls go everywhere"—an apt summary of her godless philosophy.

The early Christians took precisely the opposite view. Not only the single girl but also the single guy were supposed to refrain from all forms of extramarital intimacy. Sexual intercourse was an act reserved for the marriage bed. As we consider this strict morality, we might be tempted to picture the early Christians like the New England Puritans: elderly, somber, dark-clothed prudes who were always glaring from beneath their bristly eyebrows and wagging their fingers at the youth who just wanted to have fun. While it is certainly true that we can find some early Christians who weren't afraid to do some finger-wagging—the pamphleteer Tertullian and the fiery preacher John Chrysostom come to mind—the ancient church's view of sex wasn't just a matter of prudish legalism. Beneath the firm ethical rules was a wise, beneficial, and profoundly biblical rationale for a life of chastity.

Chastity is one of those old-fashioned words that sounds outdated but is actually very relevant. In Christian theology, chastity is contrasted with concupiscence. Both words acknowledge the biblical reality of the tumultuous desire within every person known as the "flesh." The urges of the flesh are exceedingly strong. (Did I need to inform you of that? I doubt it.) Chastity is the state of having one's fleshly urges controlled by the mind and the will, while concupiscence is the disordered state in which the flesh has free rein over the human self, resulting in chaotic and licentious actions.

Theologically, chastity can be understood as love of neighbor. A Christian does not covet the spouse who belongs to another person. Nor is the body of someone else an object for selfish gratification, for that would mean treating the person as an enemy instead of a neighbor. Chastity is also about loving oneself: Protecting one's inner sanctum, the core of one's being, the private place that ought not be exposed to the masses or be entered by anyone but a covenanted spouse.

Yet ultimately, chastity is about love of God. It is the way to experience the beauty of his presence, undistracted by false loves that would interfere. Do we not all know how the grip of concupiscence, when it has hold of us, hinders our connection to the divine? The church fathers often quoted the beatitude, "Blessed are the pure in heart, for they will see God" (Matthew 5:8). Augustine of Hippo, for example, loved this verse. He believed that the vision of God is humankind's greatest pursuit on earth, and it will be our greatest everlasting delight in heaven. What is required for humans to look upon the face of God? Jesus' answer was purity of heart. The ancient Christians took him at his word.

If you really believe this—that purification from earthly attachments will lead you to the greater pleasure of encountering God himself—then your pursuit of purification might go beyond the expected norms of society. A higher level of devotion might be required. In the ancient church, this insight began to take hold around the late third century, and it really took off in the fourth. Men and women began to choose not to get married. Instead, they pursued celibacy as a long-term lifestyle. In other words, these devoted folks wouldn't be paired up within a marriage. They wouldn't be part of a couple. They would remain as singles whose focus was worship, bodily self-denial, and Christian service. In Greek, the word for "single" or "solitary" was *monachos*. From this term, we get the English word *monk*—a person who practices the spiritual lifestyle of monasticism.

Modern Christians tend to have two main stereotypes of monks. On the one hand, monks are viewed as legalists who try to earn salvation through good works rather than faith. They wrongly endure penitential hardships to gain favor with God. The other stereotype is the hypocritical, self-indulgent monk who lives large off the fruits of the monastery despite his vows to the contrary. Often, he is a jolly fellow like Friar Tuck in the Robin Hood tales. But he isn't someone whose spiritual life you'd want to emulate.

Whether or not these stereotypes have any basis in reality—and they probably do, especially in the late medieval era—such behavior would have been abhorrent to the fervent monks of the ancient church. These men and women adopted a radical lifestyle of holy singleness because they believed that what Paul wrote in 1 Corinthians 7:25-35 was literally true. Paul claimed that "those who marry will face many troubles in this life, and I want to spare you this" (v. 28). He went on to say that married people would be divided in their attentions, but those who are unmarried had a special freedom "to be devoted to the Lord in both body and spirit" (v. 34).

For Christians today, spending one's life as a celibate single might seem like a hardship too great to bear. Yet many ancient believers didn't see things that way. Instead, they found Paul's words to ring with optimistic truth: "I am saying this for your own good, not to restrict you, but that you may live in a right way in undivided devotion to the Lord" (v. 35). What we view as an intolerable burden is actually—for those who are called to it, whether then or now—the source of life's sweetest pleasure and greatest joy.

Who Is Abstinence For?

In the early church, the monastic life was always the exception, never the norm. No matter how popular it got, no matter how many monks and nuns joined the ranks of the celibate, the majority of ancient people were married. So, if Paul's words about chastity offered an especially beautiful way "to be devoted to the Lord," was it something that most people could never know? Or was there a place for abstinence even within marriage?

Today's Christian culture tends to glorify sex within marriage. I can attest to this firsthand. When you spend as many years as I have hanging out with Christian college students, especially in informal settings like their dormitory lounges in the evenings, you pick up a few things about their views of sexuality. I recall one young man who said, "Please, Lord, don't let the Rapture happen until after I'm married!" This chaste Bible college student wanted to go to heaven as soon as possible…but not before experiencing earthly sex as well!

The Bible, of course, presents a positive view of marital sexuality. Any reader of the erotic love poetry in the Song of Songs can see that. Yet the apostle Paul once again confronts us with a counterintuitive truth: that sexual intercourse—even holy sex within marriage—can sometimes distract us from God or be a detriment to our spiritual lives. Paul writes, "Do not deprive each other except perhaps by mutual consent and for a time, so that you may devote yourselves to prayer" (1 Corinthians 7:5). Clearly, sex can sometimes be a hindrance to our necessary seasons of heightened spiritual focus. Yet the apostle warns that this abstinence should not continue indefinitely, lest it lead to temptation to stray outside of marriage.

Unfortunately, this wise Christian counsel about periodic seasons of abstinence was frequently exaggerated in the ancient church. Some believers began to disparage all sex within marriage. One extremist group called themselves the Encratites, which means "the self-controlled." They advocated total abstinence from marriage and sex. While this was a fringe movement, even some mainline Christians were influenced by similar views. We discover it especially in the popular biographies that sought to give a fuller and more vivid account of the apostles' lives. A recurring theme in those stories was chastity, not just for singles but the married as well.

For example, in the *Acts of Peter*, the supposed reason for Peter's martyrdom wasn't because of his gospel message about Christ, but because his preaching to some beautiful wives and concubines of high-ranking Roman officials taught them to leave their husbands' beds. Angered by this sudden rebuff, the powerful men conspired to order Peter's execution. Although this is nothing but apostolic legend, it does reflect what some ancient Christians believed about sex: That even within marriage, it could be a fleshly practice which should be shunned.

The debate about marriage finally drew the attention of the greatest church father, Augustine of Hippo. Too many people were criticizing marital sex, so Augustine wrote an important treatise that identified the three goods the act of marriage offers. First, it leads to procreation, the babies who will continue the human race. Second, it expresses the godly virtue of fidelity when two spouses reject all interlopers and stay exclusively committed to one another. And third, it serves as a mysterious sign (*sacramentum* was Augustine's Latin word) of a heavenly reality. When a husband and wife come together, they create a union that pictures the oneness between Christ and his church. It is important, Augustine believed, for Christ's beautiful union with his people to be sacramentally enacted by wedded spouses.

Notice that in this view, sex is not essentially about bodily enjoyment. The church fathers believed that even spouses in a marriage can indulge in concupiscence. Marital sex is lustful when it has more to do with satisfaction of the flesh than self-giving, sacrificial love—which is to say, Christlike love. Sexual intercourse should always be directed toward something higher, for it is a divine gift and should be treated as such. Of course, in the passion of the moment, this is too easy to forget. That is why periodic abstinence is a wise choice, a kind of purging of self-focus that will allow a God-focus to return.

The ancient church fathers wouldn't have liked Helen Gurley Brown's assertion that "Good girls go to heaven; bad girls go everywhere." Yet there is a nugget of truth in this foolish maxim. When badness marks your life, you really do go everywhere, casting around for something that might bring satisfaction. The impure will fail to see God with clear eyes. If that impurity is ongoing and persistent, it's worth asking whether you've ever seen God in the first place. On the other hand, those who are striving for purity through the grace of Christ—imperfectly, yet steadfastly—will be rewarded with a Beauty far greater than what any earthly infatuation could ever hope to offer.

> *It is God's will that you should be sanctified: that you should avoid*
> *sexual immorality; that each of you should learn to control your*
> *own body in a way that is holy and honorable, not in passionate*
> *lust like the pagans, who do not know God; and that in this matter*
> *no one should wrong or take advantage of a brother or sister.*
>
> 1 THESSALONIANS 4:3-6

10

Prayer Isn't a Moment;
It's a Way of Life

I remember once going to Istanbul, Turkey, and visiting the famous Blue Mosque. This magnificent building was constructed during the reign of the Ottoman Empire in the early 1600s. Its high interior dome, complex geometric decorations on the walls, and lush carpets on the floor all dazzled my eyes. But in addition to the mosque's stunning architecture, what stayed in my mind was the sight of so many devout Muslims kneeling on rugs and bowing with their faces toward Mecca.

At the time, I felt superior to these men. I didn't follow their empty ritualism—the sad and superstitious worship of a false god. Since then, however, I have been forced to ask myself some penetrating questions. Why do these followers of Allah possess such a commitment to regular prayer, while we Christians, who instead know the true God of the Bible, often treat prayer in a cavalier or discretionary way? And why do the Muslims orient their physical selves with great concern for the embodied life that we live as human beings, while modern evangelicals, who believe in the incarnation, dismiss embodied worship as a meaningless triviality?

I don't have a good answer for that. But long before Islam, the church fathers did.

The Newness of Christian Prayer

The beginning of Christian prayer came about when Jesus told his disciples, "This, then, is how you should pray" (Matthew 6:9). One of the most striking things about Jesus' prayer life was his loving intimacy with the heavenly Father. This was surprising to ancient ears. The prayers of the Jewish synagogues honored Yahweh with worship and thanked him for his many blessings. Yet the Jews didn't dare address God with such familiarity as to call him a father. Although his paternal role was acknowledged in the sense of being a protector, covenant giver, and authority figure, Yahweh couldn't be petitioned like a child coming to a delighted papa. Such intimacy was unthinkable to a first-century Jew.

Yet Jesus had no problem with it. He not only recognized God's reign in heaven and his right to be worshiped ("hallowed be thy name"), he also knew that God is a tenderhearted Father who supplies the necessary bread for each day and forgives the sins of his children. This is the exact sentiment Jesus expressed a few verses after the Lord's Prayer when he said, "Which of you, if your son asks for bread, will give him a stone? Or if he asks for a fish, will give him a snake? If you, then, though you are evil, know how to give good gifts to your children, how much more will your Father in heaven give good gifts to those who ask him!" (Matthew 7:9-11). This was a radical new way for the followers of Jesus to think about the God of the Old Testament.

But when it came to praying, the early Christians didn't only differ from the beliefs and practices of the Jews. They diverged even more from the prayers of the pagans, which weren't based on love but on divine manipulation. In such prayers, a petitioner gives something of value to a more powerful deity and gets a boon in return—basically, a religious contract between two unequal parties.

The essence of pagan prayer was captured in the Latin words *do ut des*, "I give, in order that you might give." These words were also used in contract law. Everyone recognized that prayer established a binding exchange of religious goods and services. The philosopher Plato wrote, "Is not the right way of asking [for a request from the gods] to name what we want from them?...And the right way of giving is to give them in return what they want from us...Piety is an art that the gods and men have [developed] for doing business with one another."[1] Roman religion consisted of leaving valuable offerings at a local temple in hope that the gods might grant the favor being sought or do harm to one's enemies. How different this was from early Christian prayer!

The Holy Words of Ancient Prayers

I used to teach an upper-level college course called Early Christian Thought. Before each class period, I would read a prayer from the ancient church. The students would bow their heads and pray along. Again and again, we were struck—both teacher and students—by the profundity of these ancients words. The church fathers prayed with a kind of depth, eloquence, and fervor that puts us moderns to shame. Because their prayers are so beautiful, I will share three of them here (and I wish I had space for more). Perhaps these words can become the basis for your own prayers as you commune with the saints of old.

The first prayer comes from one of the earliest church fathers, Clement of Rome, who was a pastor in that city in the late first century.

> You have opened the eyes of our heart, so that we may know you, who alone are the Most High in the heights of heaven, the Holy One among the saints. You confound the arrogance of the haughty; bring to nothing the schemes of the nations; raise up the lowly and humble the proud; enrich and impoverish; take life away and bestow it...Save all of us who are in tribulation, uplift all who have fallen, be near to those in need; heal the sick, lead back those who have wandered far from your flock; feed the hungry, liberate those who have been taken captive from out of our midst. Strengthen the weak, confirm the cowardly. Let all nations know that you are the only God, that Jesus Christ

---

1. Plato, *Euthyphro*.

is your child, and that "we are your people and the sheep of your pasture."[2]

Our second prayer comes from a man who spent most of his life as a pagan philosopher, but who converted to Christ at the end of his years. It would be as if a famous atheist like Stephen Hawking decided on his deathbed to trust Jesus. When the celebrated scholar Marius Victorinus, a long-time opponent of Christianity, came forward in an ancient church for baptism, gasps of surprise burst from the congregation, followed by great rejoicing. Here was a man who knew the true meaning of grace. Victorinus prayed:

> Have mercy on me, Lord! Christ, have mercy on me! Because God lives, because he lives eternally, eternal life has been begotten; this eternal life is Christ, the Son of God...Have mercy on me, Lord! Christ, have mercy on me! Lord, help those who have fallen! Help those who seek to rise again! Because of your divine decree and your holy judgment, even my sin has its share in the mystery of salvation. May I, at last, rest in the dwelling-place of light, saved by your grace![3]

Our third and final prayer was recorded by Paulinus of Pella at the age of 83. In a long autobiography, structured as a continuous prayer, Paulinus recalled the many trials of his life and gave thanks to God for his mercies. Then he closed his prayerful reflections like this:

> My devotion is inexhaustible; I cannot cease from rendering to you, O Christ, the homage that is your due. I know that there is one good alone that I must possess and I desire it with all my heart. It is this: that, in every place, without exception, and at all times, without excluding any, I may be able to celebrate you by my words and, in my silence, to hold you present in my mind...Whatever is reserved for

---

2. Agnes Cunningham, *Prayer: Personal & Liturgical,* vol. 16, Message of the Fathers of the Church (1985) 36–37.

3. Cunningham, *Prayer,* 71–72.

me, as my life comes to an end, may the hope of beholding you, O Christ, bring me sweet comfort. May all the doubts of anguish be dispelled by the trusting certainty, no matter where I am, that, as long as I am in this mortal body which is mine, I belong to you, to whom all things belong. May I know surely, then, that once I have been freed from all restraints of earth, I shall find life anew.[4]

As you read these godly words, let them sink into your soul. I don't know what else to say to them except, "Amen!"

The Places and Postures of Prayer

The church fathers don't just have something to teach us by the prayerful words they uttered. They also developed some specific habits they believed were important for a robust prayer life. Obviously, prayer was something that was meant to happen in church when the believers gathered on Sunday. However, praying at home should happen as well. Unlike the pagan gods whose presence was confined to their temples, the Christian God was everywhere. Therefore, he could be addressed in homes and shops as well as in formal buildings set aside for worship.

In his book *On Prayer*, the African church father Tertullian writes about the places, times, and even the bodily actions that a Christian should observe when praying. He says that a believer should pray at three intervals during the day because of the Trinity: at 9 a.m., noon, and 3 p.m. In addition, a Christian should pray at dawn and sunset. And prayers should also be said before taking a meal or a bath, since the things of heaven should precede the care of the earthly body. Tertullian adds that prayers should always be offered when a fellow Christian arrives at your home or goes on his way. What if we actually did all this?

In terms of how the body should be postured for prayer, Tertullian informs us about several early church practices. Unlike the unbelievers

---

4. Cunningham, *Prayer*, 130–31.

who approach pagan altars, a Christian's hands do not have to be specially washed, for the whole body has already been spiritually cleansed in baptism. In order to foster a spirit of humility, the hands should not be raised too high. Nor should the eyes be lifted up, but held low in deference to God's majesty (a posture that Jesus also commended in Luke 18:10-14). The voice of the person praying should be quiet, respectful, and subdued; for it is a humble heart, not the making of loud sounds, that attracts the eye of God. Though kneeling is not required, it can be a good posture as well—except on Sundays and around Easter, since this time is for rejoicing in the resurrection and isn't the right time for penitence.

Making Ancient Practice Our Own

I'd like to close this chapter with an illustration of how these ancient words of counsel have affected my own life. In my house, I have a beautiful silk rug from Turkey, the world of the Ottoman Empire. Despite its small size, the rug is expensive because it is a Hereke. These special Turkish carpets were once supplied to the palaces of the Ottoman sultans. It was given to me as a gift. Although the rug is small enough to serve as a wall hanging, I have laid it upon my floor.

Recently, during a time of spiritual testing in my life, I set the rug at my bedside. It has become a special location for me. At night before I climb into bed, I kneel in that spot to pray. Other times, I stand on that rug when I awaken and recite Isaiah 60:1-2 in my mind. This practice has consecrated a specific place to the Lord and made it, so to speak, a patch of holy ground.

I especially like that my rug sits in the liminal zone between sleeping and waking. It is the boundary between a day lived for the Lord and a good night's rest, or perhaps between my nighttime rest and a day of service to come. I certainly don't think that God credits anything to me for doing this. He isn't impressed with my little rug, nor do I receive an extra dose of spiritual merit for this practice. I just do it for myself, because the church fathers have taught me that the place and posture of prayer really do matter, and that its regular observance, day and night, should mark the life of a Christian. May the wisdom of the ancients make an impact on your prayer life as well.

*Pray in the Spirit on all occasions with all kinds of
prayers and requests. With this in mind, be alert and
always keep on praying for all the Lord's people.*

EPHESIANS 6:18

11

Invest in Your Library;
It's a Christian Thing

Clearly, you're someone who enjoys books. I know this because you're holding one made of paper. Or maybe it's on a digital reader of some kind. Or again, you might be listening to someone read this book aloud. But in any of these formats, you're encountering the words of a book. And when you do that, you're doing something special. A book is a precious thing, especially for the followers of Christ.

Christians have always recognized the importance of books. Our faith has a longstanding relationship with words on a page. Not every religion is like this, nor every culture. When European colonists first landed in the New World, the native people had no written language. They communicated solely through speech and folklore. Even today, many cultures in Africa are characterized more by orality than literacy. Usually, when Christianity comes to such lands, it fosters the invention of a script and the dissemination of written communication. This has been true from the beginning of church history. In fact, it could even be said that the early church was what made books become so widespread in the world. It's an interesting story that's well worth telling.

From Scroll to Codex

Long before the birth of Christ, the ancient Greeks had developed a love for written texts. Some would say that Western literature was begun by the Greeks, namely, by the quasi-mythical author called Homer who wrote the famous poems the *Iliad* and the *Odyssey*. By the time of the Roman Empire, the society that ringed the Mediterranean Sea was full of scribes and texts. Great literature had been composed in both Greek and Latin. But literacy wasn't just for the intellectual elites. Huge amounts of crude graffiti and scrawled notes on discarded pieces of pottery prove that many commoners could read and write as well. Literacy, at least at a basic level, was a big part of Greco-Roman culture.

The Jews, too, had been literate for a long time. We know this because they produced the Old Testament, along with many other texts in Hebrew and Greek. The synagogues of the first century made a point of teaching the Torah to the boys of the surrounding area. Jesus was taught to read in such a setting (Luke 4:16; John 7:15). Thus, the background cultures of early Christianity—the Jews, the Greeks, and the Romans—had already adopted written communication when the new faith arrived on the scene.

But what exactly were people reading in those days? In other words, what did they have in their hands when they read a "text"? In the first century, this would have meant one of two things. Some texts were written on wax tablets. These were wooden frames filled with soft wax that could be scratched with a sharp pen to make letters. Such texts were transient by nature, for they could be easily erased by smoothing the wax with the blunt end of the pen.

For more important and longer-lasting texts, ancient authors used scrolls. The most common material was a mesh made from the pith of the papyrus plant. It was pressed into a single sheet and dried into something like paper. Then the sheets were glued into a long, continuous roll. The other material for scrolls was parchment made from the skin of sheep or goats. Basically, it was leather that had been scraped, smoothed, and whitened into a suitable writing surface.

The drawbacks to these writing media are obvious. Wax tablets were too unstable for important texts. One wrong thumbprint and you could lose a key word—and you don't even want to think about what a hot day might do! Ink on papyrus or parchment was much more permanent. Yet scrolls had their own weaknesses. Have you ever wrapped a large present for Christmas? Then you know how hard it can be to maneuver a big roll of paper. Scrolls required a great deal of effort to find the place you wanted. You couldn't unroll the whole thing at once. You had to wind up one stick as you unspooled the other. "I'd sure like to compare this passage to the one I read an hour ago," you might think as you encountered an interesting paragraph. Too bad. The previous one was now buried under 30 feet of brittle paper or leather. That's as high as a three-story building! Scrolls were cumbersome to handle, and they didn't let you move easily through a whole document.

Conveniently, though, wax tablets would let you do exactly that. Scribes, clerks, or even schoolboys would bind several tablets together with thongs to form a clunky kind of book. This gave readers the advantage of being able to flip back and forth between the tablets. Writers could put a text or a list of business transactions on several tablets and keep the whole thing bound into a single volume. Quite handy, when you think about it.

But let's take it a step further. What if you combined the advantages of both methods and connected some leaves of parchment with stitching along one edge? Of course, you'd need a sturdy cover to protect the fragile pages. But after putting all this together, you'd have a document that is easy to carry around and peruse at your leisure. Sometime in the first century AD, this method was tried, and it worked quite well. Coincidentally, this was the same moment the apostles were starting to write letters and record biographies of Jesus' life. The Christians found that this new writing method—called a *codex*—was exactly what they needed. They quickly abandoned the scrolls that the Jews had used in their synagogues (and still do today). The age of the book had dawned, and the ancient Christians adopted this new writing medium with enthusiasm.

In addition to its portability and ease of use, a codex had an important economic advantage over scrolls. This advantage will be obvious to any landlord who has unoccupied rooms in his building, or to a property owner who has vacant lots waiting to be developed. Every businessman understands the value of using capacity that is owned but hasn't yet been exploited. With a writing surface, what is this unused resource? The back of the page! You can't flip over a thirty-foot roll and put writing there. But that is exactly what you can do with a codex. The new medium allowed publishers to double the amount of letters that each piece of expensive parchment could contain. Using cheaper papyrus would bring down the costs even more. This meant that books were a much more affordable format than scrolls, a welcome benefit for the Christians who usually weren't from the rich aristocracy.

Although the historical period we are discussing is the ancient era, we should note that Christianity continued its love affair with books right into modern times. When the Roman Empire fell to Germanic invaders, it was the Christians—especially the scholars and scribes who took refuge on the isolated island of Ireland—who preserved not only theological books, but the entire legacy of Greco-Roman literature. In the Middle Ages, Christian monks were the primary transmitters of written texts. And when Johannes Gutenberg invented his printing press in the 1400s, the Protestant Reformers widely adopted the new technology. Christian book publishers have been flourishing ever since—including the one founded in 1974 that brought you the book you're now reading!

The Reason for Ancient Books

So far we have seen that the ancient Christians were early adopters of the codex, but we haven't really discussed why (other than economics and practicality). What was it about Christianity—at a deeper level—that made books so central and important? I will suggest four reasons.

First, the early Christians were united into a single community. In chapter 4 we saw the importance they placed on their interconnectedness, which they called catholicity. A Christian congregation in one city felt intimately bound to all the rest. Everyone was part of the whole body of Christ. The pagan religion didn't function that way. A follower of Jupiter in Rome didn't feel a spiritual bond with a devotee of Artemis in Ephesus. But the Christians operated exactly like this, which meant they needed to exchange messages between one another. This certainly included personal letters (such as the epistles of the New Testament). Yet it also included devotional texts that one congregation found beneficial and wanted to share. Admittedly, the Christians weren't alone in their love for sharing religious texts. The Gnostics also did this, and so did the new, more communal cults called "mystery religions." Yet it was the Christians who emphasized books more than anyone else. One church father, Origen of Alexandria, needed a staff of more than 15 stenographers and copyists, as well as a host of girls trained in calligraphy, to take down all the books that poured from his mind! Christians have always felt compelled to encourage one another with good books.

The second important reason for the church fathers' adoption of books was their emphasis on making truth claims. Here again, paganism wasn't like this. Theological teachings formed no part of Greco-Roman religion. For the pagans, it didn't matter what you believed, but what you did. The gods watched your rituals and behaviors closely. If they liked what they saw, they blessed you. If you got it wrong, watch out. But Christians were devoted to what came to be called *orthodoxy*, or "right belief." It truly mattered whether you believed that Jesus was God in the flesh, or that he literally rose from the dead, or that he was coming back to bring judgment and rewards. People who believed a specific set of truths—the good news—received salvation, while those who rejected those claims would perish forever. In order to spread ideas far and wide without errors or mistakes, written texts are required. The game of "telephone" doesn't cut it when it comes to Christian proclamation, for the message will soon spin out of control. Only a book can fix truth in indelible ink, then transmit those ideas to the uttermost ends of the earth.

The historical nature of the Christian faith was a third motivator for adopting books. The Jews had set the precedent for this. Judaism didn't propagate myths and fables about the doings on faraway Mount Olympus. They cared about God's earthly deeds for the sake of his chosen people. The historical stories of Abraham, Moses, the Exodus, and the good or bad judges and kings of Israel were all recorded in the Old Testament. This same perspective motivated the early Christians to record the amazing works of the Savior and the church's subsequent history. As Luke explained to his patron, "Since I myself have carefully investigated everything from the beginning, I too decided to write an orderly account for you, most excellent Theophilus, so that you may know the certainty of the things you have been taught" (Luke 1:3-4). Later, the brave deeds of the martyrs also compelled the Christians to record eyewitness accounts, lest the memories of such heroic feats ever be forgotten. Books were the means by which accurate records could be maintained so all the churches could know what God was up to in the world.

We would be remiss if we didn't mention the fourth and most basic reason the early Christians valued books. It is a theological reason—one that is at the core of Christianity. John the apostle summed it up when his Gospel announced, "In the beginning was the Word" (John 1:1). Think about the profundity of this statement. The essence of God is to possess a message within himself. In the Holy Trinity, the Father is the speaker, the Son is the spoken word, and the Spirit is the breath by which the speaker speaks. The universe came into existence through a divine word: "And God said, 'Let there be light'" (Genesis 1:3). It is the Father's nature to speak forth saving words (Psalm 107:20; 119:105; Hebrews 4:12). It is the Son's nature to be the Word made flesh (John 1:14; Hebrews 1:1-2). And it is the Spirit's nature to illumine human minds into the meaning of what God has spoken (John 16:13; 1 Corinthians 2:13-14).

Hear the Word of the Lord

The ancient church had a pastoral office that few churches still have today. This person was called a *lector*, literally, a reader. His job was to stand up in church and read the Scriptures aloud. The lections weren't just short snippets of the Bible, but large portions drawn from both Testaments. Such readings took a long time to proclaim. Sometimes the accounts of martyrs or other holy people were read aloud as well.

We might wonder: Isn't this a waste of time? Why not just read a summary and get on to the real business of life application? Don't we come to church for the practical takeaways that can help us live better? Although we might suppose so today, the ancient church didn't think that way. They knew the Word of God was living and active, sharper than a soldier's sword. It was a text worth sitting in for a long time, receiving it like refreshing streams of water, like sweet honeycombs, like medicine for the soul. When you really believe in the power of words, you gravitate toward written documents. They're the best way to get God's truth into as many hands—and hearts—as possible. The ancients remind us that to be a lover of God is to be a lover of books.

Keep this Book of the Law always on your lips; meditate on it day and night, so that you may be careful to do everything written in it.

Joshua 1:8

12

Every Good Story
Has Three Acts

I n our last chapter, we saw how the early Christians celebrated books.
In this one, we'll discover what they put into their books. It was the
greatest story ever told. And it had three essential parts: Old Testament,
New Testament, and the age to come.

Stories have been divided into three acts since time immemorial.
The earliest surviving work on dramatic structure is a book by the
Greek philosopher Aristotle, which he called *Poetics*. This isn't just a
book about poetry, but all kinds of storytelling in literature. Aristotle
puts it like this: "Let us now discuss the proper structure of the plot,
since this is the first and most important thing in [a story]...A whole
[story] is that which has a beginning, a middle, and an end." He goes
on to explain that the beginning is the part that doesn't arise from
something else, while the end is the part that naturally follows from
what came before. The middle, of course, follows from one thing yet
is also followed by something else. "A well constructed plot," Aristotle
concludes, "must neither begin nor end haphazardly, but must con-
form to these principles."[1]

This ancient Greek philosopher got it exactly right. The best stories

---

1. Aristotle, *Poetics* 7 (1450b).

always burst onto the scene without a lot of clunky verbiage to set the stage. In Act 1, you get to know the main characters, both good and bad. Soon a problem arises that the good guys will try to overcome and the bad guys will seek to make worse. This is known in literary theory as "rising action." The initial problem builds to a climax that must be resolved in one way or another. Act 3 is where the resolution happens. The story must end with a bang.

What about the middle? Novelists and playwrights always fear Act 2. It is typically the longest act, maybe twice as long as the other two. The fear is that there's nothing to say here, no real story to tell, so the characters will just muddle along until the climax. But that never works. In the three-act plot structure, there must be intensifying conflict and meaningful advancement toward the last battle. This is the art of storytelling. Nobody would have liked *Star Wars* if Luke Skywalker had spent the whole time between Tatooine and the Death Star polishing his lightsaber and having coffee at a galactic Starbucks. A good story will have a dynamic beginning, a meaningful middle, and a satisfying end.

The Christian Metanarrative

Another term literary theorists use is *metanarrative*. The prefix *meta-* creates the idea of an overarching storyline that encompasses lesser stories into the grand, defining one. For example, the individual stories of native peoples, fur trappers, pioneer settlers, and cowboys all fit into a metanarrative of America's westward expansion. Most nations have foundational myths like this: the stories that define who the people are, where they came from, and where they're headed. The Bible has a metanarrative too. Or better, we can say that God has a metanarrative, for he is the author of history. And in the great historical tale that God is telling, he has ordained a beginning, a middle, and an end.

The ancient church fathers knew they were in the middle of something big. Jesus Christ wasn't just the founder of a new entity called the church. He also stood in the train of Israel's prophets before him. Jesus was the culmination of the mighty work that God had been doing since the creation of Adam. In fact, Jesus was even understood as the centerpiece of cosmic history from the creation of the world to its fiery end. This idea is biblical. In Ephesians 1:8-10, Paul writes, "With all wisdom and understanding, [God] made known to us the mystery… which he purposed in Christ, to be put into effect when the times reach their fulfillment—to bring unity to all things in heaven and on earth under Christ."

Let us pause and consider Paul's expression, "to bring unity to all things." In Greek, the word is significant: *anakephalaioō*. This is made up of two terms. The root word *kephalē* means "head," while the prefix *ana-* means "again." So this verb means "to head up again," that is, to reorder everything under its proper heading so that all is unified and orderly like it should be. Our English word that means the same thing (based on Latin) is *recapitulation*. (*Capitalis* means "of the head," as in a state capital, or capital punishment.) Whether it was the Greek-speaking fathers or the Latin, they understood this biblical term to be saying something important about the scope of history: it was being written in orderly sequence by the pen of God, who is the master storyteller.

Irenaeus, bishop of Lyon in France in the late second century, is noted for his theology of recapitulation. At the risk of overwhelming you with verbiage, I am going to quote a long but important passage from his work *Against Heresies*. You will notice Irenaeus's quotation of Ephesians 1:10 at the end of it. It runs,

> The church, although dispersed throughout the whole world, even to the ends of the earth, has received from the apostles and their disciples this faith: [We believe] in one God the Father Almighty, maker of heaven and earth, and the sea, and all things that are in them; and in one Jesus Christ, the Son of God, who became incarnate for our salvation; and in the Holy Spirit, who proclaimed through the prophets the dispensations of God and [Christ's] advents; and the birth from a virgin; and the passion; and the resurrection from the dead; and the bodily ascension into heaven of the beloved Jesus Christ,

our Lord; and His [future] manifestation from heaven in the glory of the Father "to gather all things in one," and to raise up anew all flesh of the whole human race, in order that to Jesus Christ our Lord, and God, and Savior, and King, according to the will of the invisible Father, "every knee should bow, things in heaven, and things on earth, and things under the earth."[2]

Perhaps the first thing you might notice about this quotation is that it sounds a lot like the Apostles' Creed. And indeed, this is an example of what the creed looked like in Irenaeus's time, before it had assumed the fixed wording that modern churches use. Yet notice his larger point. Scholars have noted that Irenaeus is telling a story here. He is recounting a cosmic, Christ-centered metanarrative of creation, prediction, incarnation, crucifixion, resurrection, ascension, and consummation. Christianity is not just a bullet-point list of dogmas that must be believed. It is not mere head knowledge. No, theology is narrative. Doctrine is story. History is plotline. Christians are protagonists in a drama. Our deeds are dramatic actions that unfold on the stage as we play our roles in God's grand theater.

Don't miss the structure of the metanarrative that Irenaeus is describing in the quotation above. For him, there was an Act 1, when God created the world and sent forth his prophets. Now we are in Act 2, when Christ has come and we are living in the time between the times. Christians must always be second-act people. Never should we long for the past, be obsessed with the present, or be unmindful of the future. Instead we must remember the past and engage wisely with the present. And always, we must steadfastly believe in a soon-to-come Act 3, when the climax of history will be reached. Then the last battle will be fought and Jesus will stand as victor. Satan will be vanquished, his throne will be relinquished, and death will be extinguished. Finally, all things will be recapitulated in the Lord Jesus Christ.

Who wouldn't want to play a role in a story like that? Well, as it turns out, a lot of ancient people didn't. Many of them wanted to cling

---

2. Irenaeus, *Against Heresies* 1.10.1.

to their timeworn myths, the old stories of gods who were clearly acting out a different plotline. Other so-called Christians—but heretics, really—wanted to tell a similar-sounding story to the biblical one, yet falsify it at key points. It's like one of those remake movies that is supposedly based on Shakespeare, but it runs off in crazy directions that the Bard never intended. Movies like that are Shakespearean in their concept and characters; yet upon closer inspection, they're different stories entirely. Back in ancient church times, one heretic in particular told a pseudo-Christian story like this. His name was Marcion, and it's now time to take a closer look at this teller of counterfeit tales.

The Creator and His Christ

Marcion of Sinope was a rich businessman who made his fortune in shipping on the Black Sea. In the middle of the second century, he came to Rome and gave a huge donation to the church. At first, he was accepted as a prominent Christian leader, until the locals actually got to know what he was teaching. As we've already noted in chapter 4, Marcion believed that everything Jewish must be purged from Christianity. The Old Testament, he declared, had nothing to do with Christ. Anything Jewish in the New Testament had been falsified by misguided apostles. It had to be cut away to restore the true Gentile core. One of Marcion's main works was called *Antitheses*, in which he made a long list of the contradictions between the Old Testament and the New.

The reason Marcion felt this way was because Yahweh seemed to be very different from the Father God whom Jesus talked about. Marcion had decided that they must be two separate gods. One was an incompetent, volatile, and cruel deity of the Israelites who could be ignored. He was the foolish creator who had made this messed-up world. However, Jesus had come to tell us about another god who overlooked our sins without faulting us, brushing them under the rug because he loved us. He simply declared that we were all forgiven. Thus we are free from having to do legalistic works. We serve the good god in gratitude instead of fear. Some of these ideas have a ring of truth to them, since the apostle Paul did distinguish between the Jewish Law and the gospel of grace. We are, in fact, saved by faith and not by works. But Marcion took things much further than Paul ever did; he kicked the Old Testament God out of Christianity altogether.

What does Marcion's plotline do to the Christian metanarrative? It destroys it by splitting it in two. His story has the same characters as the orthodox one. But the plotline is rearranged, forcing the characters into very different roles. Ultimately, it separates the creator God from his Christ—exactly the opposite of what the creeds had always declared. The church fathers saw this immediately. The Roman church's leaders refunded Marcion's donation and excommunicated him. And down in Africa, the prolific writer Tertullian began to compose a massive, five-volume work against these dangerous ideas. Marcion had gathered a wide following, and he needed to be refuted.

Tertullian employed the same argument as Irenaeus (who lived shortly before him): That the biblical story of Christianity, which is summarized in the church's creeds, does not allow the church's Jewish origins to be rejected. On the contrary, the era of the Old Testament is Act 1 of a three-act play. The saga of ancient Israel launched the storyline that Jesus entered when he became incarnate in Act 2. He was the Jewish son of Jewish parents, the Messiah who had come to set Israel free. Praise be to the one God, the wild olive branch of the Gentiles was grafted into the Jewish tree that had already been planted (Romans 11:11-24; Ephesians 2:14). Together, both Jew and Gentile— all who believed in the Messiah—would become the one people of God. Then the end of time would come, when the Suffering Servant would become the Conquering King. All enemies would be defeated. The 12 tribes of Israel and the 12 apostles of Christ would be united. And the story would be complete.

By the time Irenaeus and Tertullian were done writing, the Marcionites were on their way out. No longer would Marcion's bifurcated view be a viable option. But beyond this antiheretical victory, something even more important had been achieved. Christianity had become firmly established as a three-act play. The two Testaments of Scripture had been united into a single story that hinged on Jesus Christ. A deeper and more cohesive theology of salvation history had been bequeathed to the church. Today, we are characters within that ongoing saga. We do not know when the story will culminate, or exactly how. Yet there's one thing of which we're certain. We know who is going to win at the end.

I am the Alpha and the Omega, the First and
the Last, the Beginning and the End.

Revelation 22:13

13

The Bible Can't Be Taken Literally

U h-oh. I can feel it. The maxim above has put your heresy radar on full alert. "I knew it would happen," you're saying to yourself. "Litfin's book was teaching me some good lessons. But here's where it goes off the rails. I knew it would happen sooner or later. The church fathers have led this guy astray."

No, hang with me. We are still squarely on the rails. You can still trust the church fathers to lead you into wisdom, even when they're urging you not to take the Bible literally. I am going to try and make that case to you now. It's all about definitions.

Let's begin with the word *literal*. It is the opposite of terms like *figurative, metaphorical,* or *symbolic*. We tend to make this terminology hinge on whether or not something is *true*. Things that are literally true are reliable and real, while symbolic statements have diminished truth value, or maybe aren't even true at all. But literalism doesn't have to be the only way to truth. Sometimes you need symbols to show you truth in a different way. In fact, there are times when an allegory can speak truth even more clearly than literalism.

C.S. Lewis certainly understood this. His Narnia novels are masterpieces of Christian allegory. When Susan and Lucy contemplate the shorn and slain Aslan on the Stone Table, then witness him come alive again, they can teach us more theological truth than many a dusty book of doctrine. That is why Lewis said, "The function of allegory is not to hide but to reveal, and it is properly used only for that which cannot be said, or so well said, in literal speech. The inner life, and specially the life of love, religion, and spiritual adventure, has therefore always been the field of true allegory."[1]

The Letter and the Spirit

The ancient church fathers held pure literalism in suspicion. This wasn't because they wanted to avoid the literal meaning of the text so they could foist their own meanings onto Scripture. Rather, they were concerned that if interpreters stayed only at the level of the written letters (which is what *literal* literally means), the Christian church would overlook truths about Jesus on every page of the Bible. There had to be Christological content underneath the letters, even if it wasn't apparent on a purely literal reading. And who was the first biblical interpreter to make this point? His name might surprise you. It was the apostle Paul.

In 2 Corinthians 3, Paul addresses two covenants or ministry arrangements: the old one set up under the Jewish Law, and the more glorious one that had been ushered in by Christ. In this context, he makes a bold statement in verse 6: "The letter kills, but the Spirit gives life." Paul goes on to explain that interpreters have a grievous problem when they approach the Bible like his Jewish adversaries do. They can only read the letters but they can't discern the deeper meaning. Their minds have been dulled. A veil stands between them and the truth—and "only in Christ is it taken away. Even to this day when Moses is read, a veil covers their hearts. But whenever anyone turns to the Lord, the veil is taken away" (vv. 14-16). Then, and only then, can an interpreter see the true, Christian meaning of the Bible.

Another passage from Paul tells us how this Christ-centered interpretation is supposed to work. In Galatians 4:21-31, the apostle is once again contrasting the old Jewish covenant and the new covenant of

---

1. C.S. Lewis, *The Allegory of Love: A Study in Medieval Tradition* (1936), 166.

Christ. He speaks of the two mothers of Abraham's sons, Sarah and Hagar. One was a slave woman, the other free. Paul declares that those who are in Hagar's lineage are slaves themselves. They are of the flesh and live in an earthly Jerusalem. However, the heirs of Sarah (i.e., the Christians) are free people, the children of a divine promise who dwell in a celestial Jerusalem.

Now if you go back and look at the Sarah and Hagar narratives in Genesis 16 and 21, you will not find these concepts discussed there. Certainly you will find no explicit mention of Christ. Instead, you will find a tragic story of an enslaved handmaiden who was cast out of Abraham's home along with her son, Ishmael. Yet they both received mercy from God. That is the literal story in Genesis, and there are important truths to be derived from it. But Paul insists—under the inspiration of the Holy Spirit—that there is another interpretive layer. "These things are being taken figuratively," he says. "The women represent two covenants" (Galatians 4:24).

What is Paul's Greek word that is translated as "figuratively"? It is the verb *allēgoreō*, which means "to say something else in addition." That is what allegory does. The letter of the text says one thing, then allegory adds another layer of truth. This is a useful interpretive approach when you are uncovering truths that are actually meant to be found. But of course, allegory might also be used to inject wild speculations into the biblical text, ideas that aren't drawn from the passage but from one's own imagination. This was the quandary the church fathers faced when they approached the multilayered pages of God's Word. There had to be more under the surface, more Christology than the Jews were willing to allow. Yet not every interpretation that anyone could think up was valid. What kind of interpretive boundaries would prevent dangerous flights of fancy?

Alexandria and Antioch

In the ancient church, two main schools of thought developed around these ideas. One was located in the Egyptian city of Alexandria. This was a very intellectual place—the Harvard of the ancient world.

The foremost Bible interpreter in the Alexandrian school was a brilliant scholar named Origen (AD 185–254). He was a rigorous and austere man, profoundly affected by the death of his father as a martyr. He was also affected by the intellectual culture of his great city. Greek philosophy was widely studied there. Like so many of the church fathers, Origen found himself especially drawn to Platonism.

Unfortunately, Origen bought into Platonism a little too much. He went beyond what we saw in chapter 6, when Justin Martyr contextualized the Christian faith in Platonic language that his culture could understand. Though I respect Origen's achievements very much, I think it's fair to say that he melded Christianity and Platonism in ways that went beyond what the Bible actually taught. This fusion caused him to say some sketchy things that even his contemporaries found troublesome.

One of these difficulties was Origen's view of the Bible's literal text. Platonism took a negative view of anything physical or earthly. For the Platonists, truth only existed in the world above where everything was pure and eternal. When this outlook was grafted onto the Pauline distinction between letter and spirit, Origen was led to give too little value to the literal and historical meaning of Scripture. He had become tainted by his Platonic presuppositions, which emphasized distant, spiritual truths instead of concrete realities.

This does not mean Origen ignored the biblical words themselves. Far from it! No one in the ancient church studied Hebrew and Greek in greater detail (or with greater affection) than this man. One of his greatest works was the *Hexapla*, a side-by-side comparison of various Bible translations in six columns. Imagine doing that in the days before computers or printing presses. Back then, cutting and pasting still involved scissors and glue! Origen was a man who loved the words of the Bible with an ardor rarely matched in church history.

The problem came when Origen encountered literal interpretations that he didn't think were "worthy of God." All of us have encountered verses like this. If we are honest, the Bible often throws us for a loop, especially in the Old Testament. Whenever Origen ran into problematic texts, he resorted to the ever-ready tool of allegory. The Bible, he believed, contained intentional stumbling blocks that were injected into the literal sense by Christ himself. The wise interpreter was supposed to notice them and start looking for a symbolic meaning instead. Regrettably, Origen went to the well of allegory too often. He started uncovering all kinds of hidden things in the Bible's pages. Normally, his discoveries were acceptably pious, even if they weren't what Moses or David or Jeremiah ever had in mind. But occasionally Origen ran out on a limb with more speculative and radical ideas. People began to take notice of this, and not with approval. The main school that criticized Origen arose in Antioch.

The Antiochian church fathers pulled back to a more literal understanding of the Bible. However, they still rejected the kind of literalism that prevented any Christological meaning from being found in the Old Testament. Christ-centered interpretation had to happen, said the Antiochians, just not with the kind of free-for-all that Origen's allegory allowed. Alexandrian allegory was too easy to abuse.

Instead of using that troublesome term, the Antiochian school preferred to speak of "theorizing." In this method, spiritual truth had to be drawn directly from the literal sense. One of this school's leaders, Diodore, was a bishop in Paul's hometown of Tarsus (which wasn't far from Antioch). Diodore of Tarsus wrote, "We will not shrink from the truth but will expound it according to the historical substance and the plain literal sense...One thing is to be watched, however: theorizing must never be understood as doing away with the underlying sense; it would then no longer be theorizing but allegory."[2] The Antiochians staked out a claim to an interpretive method that was less extravagant than Alexandria's. They would only build their interpretations off of the literal sense, not introducing foreign ideas as allegory sometimes allowed. Yet both schools insisted that Christ must be found in the Old Testament. This was a hallmark of early Christian biblical interpretation.

Why did the church fathers insist on this principle? It was really no more than what Jesus himself had said. In chapter 5 of John's Gospel, we see Jesus being persecuted by the Jewish leaders for his teachings. They

---

2. Karlfried Froehlich, *Biblical Interpretation in the Early Church* (1984) 85.

were even trying to kill him for breaking the Sabbath. But Jesus was having none of it. These learned men who supposedly knew the Law of Moses were actually blind to what it had been telling them. They couldn't see that Jesus was the fulfillment of everything the Law was about.

Jesus called out these rabbis with a firm rebuke. "You have never heard [God's] voice nor seen his form," he told these false leaders of Israel, "nor does his word dwell in you, for you do not believe the one he sent. You study the Scriptures diligently because you think that in them you have eternal life. These are the very Scriptures that testify about me, yet you refuse to come to me to have life…If you believed Moses, you would believe me, for he wrote about me" (John 5:37-39,46).

The church fathers paid close attention to these words. They saw how firmly Jesus declared that Moses wrote about him—not just here and there in a few prophecies, but throughout the Scriptures. If you read the Old Testament with extreme literalism, you will only find Jewish history, wisdom, and law. However, if you read the Bible like a Christian—filled with the Holy Spirit who has removed the veil from your eyes—you will see that Jesus is the subject and goal of every passage. Instead of strict literalism, there must be a willingness to let the Bible "say something else" about Jesus. This is a point of wisdom from the ancient church that we often miss today.

As I said at the outset of this chapter, I am no heretic or Bible-denier. Yet I cannot recommend that you read the Bible "literally," as if it is a just a sterile record of long-ago events. No, the Bible is so much more than a historical document from ancient Israel. The Word of God always points us to the incarnate Word who is its subject. So the next time you open the Bible, let the veil slip away as you contemplate the Savior from Genesis to Revelation.

*"How foolish you are, and how slow to believe all that the
prophets have spoken! Did not the Messiah have to suffer
these things and then enter his glory?" And beginning
with Moses and all the Prophets, he explained to them
what was said in all the Scriptures concerning himself.*

LUKE 24:25-27

14

What You Say Out Loud
Is What You Believe

Can you be a true Christian and never say so out loud? It's an inter-esting question, isn't it? Few people would ever do this—believe in Christ yet never tell a soul—so it's probably just a theoretical question.

Perhaps, however, such a thing might happen in the context of persecution. A believer might stay underground for his or her whole life. For example, in the profound and disturbing film *Silence*, three seventeenth-century Jesuit missionaries attempt to convert the Japanese people to Christianity.[1] Because of terrible pressures and tortures, Rodrigues, one of the missionaries, denies his faith. He blasphemes Jesus and helps the Japanese government restrict Christianity for many years. However, at Rodrigues's Buddhist funeral at the end of his long life, he is shown by filmmaker Martin Scorsese in the process of being cremated. The camera zooms in and reveals that the corpse of Rodrigues is holding a tiny crucifix, placed there by his wife—the very crucifix that he had received when he first arrived in Japan. Did this man secretly retain his faith in Christ for several decades, even though he quit confessing it in any discernable way?

I don't claim to have the answer to such a difficult question. Who

---

1. The film is based upon the novel *Silence* by Shūsaku Endō.

can say what any of us would do when subjected to unbearable pressure or physical trauma? Only God knows if someone's faith is genuine. What I do know is this: Verbal confession is an essential part of Christianity. I say this confidently because it doesn't require me to rely on things I can't know, like the state of someone else's soul. This truth comes directly from the Word of God. Christians are commanded to confess the true faith, and that includes speaking it out loud.

Confess the Faith

The biblical term *confession* is one of those theological words that carries a lot of weight but is often overlooked. The Greek noun is *homologia*, and of course, it has a verb form as well ("to confess"). We tend to think of this word only in one of its several possible meanings. Confession, for us, usually means telling God or others about our sins. This is how the word functions, for example, in 1 John 1:9, which reminds us that if we confess our sins, God faithfully forgives them.

But let's drill deeper into this word, because it's important for the point I want to make in this chapter. In Greek, the prefix *homo-* means "same," while the word for a "saying" is a *logion*. So a confession is a "same-saying," that is, agreement. You can see how this works when confessing your sins. You are no longer excusing them but finally saying the same thing that God would say: that you've done wrong. You have come to the point where you aren't denying your guilt but agreeing about the sin and asking God to forgive you. This is certainly one aspect of confession.

Yet the Bible uses the term *confession* in other ways too. Anytime we confess something, we "same-say" what God has already said. We proclaim out loud the very words of God, acknowledging them as true because they came from him. This is how the term functions in Romans 10:9-10, which is the passage I had in mind when I said above that verbal confession is essential to Christianity.

In Romans 10, Paul is addressing what a person must do in order to be saved. His answer is clear: "If you confess (*homologeō*) with your mouth that Jesus is Lord and believe in your heart that God raised him from the dead, you will be saved. For with the heart one believes and is justified, and with the mouth one confesses (*homologeō*) and is saved" (ESV). Look at this passage closely. The mouth and the heart go together. It's not enough just to have an inner disposition of faith. My friends, you gotta say it out loud. Faith speaks up, or it isn't faith at all.

But what, exactly, must be believed and uttered aloud to receive salvation? Though we tend to make the gospel so complicated, the Bible actually keeps it rather simple. Think back to chapter 1 of this book. We have already identified the core thing that must be believed by a Christian for salvation. It is the three-word gospel (or just two in Greek): "Jesus is Lord." We saw in chapter 1 that this simple statement embraced the truth that although Jesus had been crucified, he was then raised from the dead by the power of God, making him the glorious Lord who is exalted to the Father's right hand. The apostle Peter summarized the gospel like this: "God has made him both Lord and Christ, this Jesus whom you crucified" (Acts 2:36 ESV).

"Christian, What Do You Believe?"

The lordship of Christ was the core confession of the early Christians, and they said it often. In the phrase "Jesus is Lord" and a few other expressions about him, we have the beginnings of what we know today as creeds. They are scattered throughout the New Testament (e.g., Romans 1:2-4; 1 Timothy 3:16). Sometimes, these creeds had two parts, describing the Father God and his Christ (1 Corinthians 8:6; 1 Timothy 6:13). More rarely, they included the Holy Spirit as well, and so were threefold (2 Corinthians 13:14).

The most important of these primitive creeds is found in 1 Corinthians 15:3-6. The apostle Paul records the summary of the Christian faith that he was taught immediately after his conversion: that Christ died for sins and rose from the dead before many witnesses. Since Paul is quoting something very early here—the foundational creed of the Jerusalem church—it means these are the first Christian words of which we have any record, preceding the writing of any other New Testament words by several years. This confession of faith expresses what Christians have believed from the very beginning.

During the second and third centuries, the more primitive creeds of the New Testament came together into a Christological summary that the ancients called the "rule of faith." The wording of this formula wasn't fixed, nor was its content always exactly the same. Yet its narrative flow was consistent, making it recognizable whenever the church fathers quoted it. This ancient formula covered the whole Christian story from start to finish: *creation* of the world by God, *prediction* of the Messiah by the prophets, his *incarnation* by the Virgin Mary, his *crucifixion* by Pontius Pilate, his *resurrection* from the grave, his *ascension* to the Father's right hand, the *proclamation* of the gospel by the church, and the *consummation* of history at the Lord's return for judgment and rewards.

By the fourth century, the language of these confessions had become more fixed—not rigidly the same throughout the empire, yet often incorporating the same basic wording among all Christians. One of the most important of these formulas is called the Old Roman Symbol (*symbolon* was an ancient word for a creed, originally referring to a password that soldiers used to prove they belonged to the troop). We have this Old Roman Symbol preserved in both Greek and Latin. Over the centuries, the text was adapted until it finally assumed a common, shared form that all Latin-speaking Christians used. Today it is known as the Apostles' Creed, and it is recited by many Christians every Sunday. Its first word is *credo*, "I believe," which is where we get our English term, *creed*.

In addition to the Apostles' Creed, there are two others that were articulated in ancient councils instead of evolving gradually in the churches over time. The first of these is the Nicene Creed, composed at the Council of Nicaea in AD 325 (updated and finalized in 381). It defines the doctrine of the Trinity, which we will explore in chapter 23. The other is the so-called Chalcedonian Definition, which comes from the Council of Chalcedon in 451. It covers the perfect balance of Christ's deity and humanity, which will be our topic in chapter 24.

The Ancient Use of Creeds

Christians who use creeds today assume they belong in a dry environment. But they didn't start out that way. Originally, creeds were wet. *Huh? Creeds were wet?* What I'm saying is this: The original place where creeds were used wasn't the regular Sunday service, when everyone was gathered for Scripture readings, a sermon, and the Lord's Supper. Instead, creeds were originally used in the service of baptism—literally down in the font—when the convert went underwater with the creed on his lips and came out again in newness of life. Ancient creeds emerged in the context of baptism. How come?

Remember that the society of the early Christians had a completely pagan outlook that was ignorant of a biblical perspective. So when someone converted to Christianity, they weren't just making a switch of religions while keeping everything else the same. They were leaving a complete and total worldview in order to enter another one. In fact, they were leaving one cosmic metanarrative—the myths of the pagan gods that explained how the universe worked—to enter the Christian story as characters within God's glorious drama (as we saw in chapter 12).

Upon believing in the Savior of the world, these former pagans were instructed in the things of Christ. They had to be taught the doctrinal content of the faith and the moral requirements of God—things that were brand new to them. They weren't familiar with Christian principles at all. Such baby Christians needed deep instruction before they could be baptized. This process was called catechesis. We will discuss it more fully in the next chapter.[2]

Although creeds began as verbal confessions that were spoken aloud in the waters of baptism after an extensive period of instruction, the church fathers quickly realized that creeds could have other uses too. One was to serve as a guide in biblical interpretation. In those days, heretics often claimed that the biblical story was different than the one we know. In response, some of the church fathers looked to the ancient rule of faith to articulate the overarching plotline of Scripture. With that summary as a guide, they could show what the Bible was really saying—and reject the nonsense of heretics.

---

2. The reason I keep referring to other chapters in this book is because there's an interconnected unity to what I'm saying about the ancient church. I want you to see how it all hangs together!

Over time, the "wet" creeds of the first few centuries also began to serve their "dry" purpose that I mentioned above. As the liturgy of the church became more formalized in the fourth century and beyond, creeds were incorporated into the weekly doctrinal affirmation for the gathered faithful. In particular, the Nicene Creed became a standard part of what Christians recited in the church service. It is no exaggeration to say that ever since the fifth century, there has never been a Sunday when the Nicene Creed hasn't been spoken aloud by some congregation of Christians somewhere in the world. That's an amazing thought!

Among Western Christians, the Apostles' Creed also has been widely recited. However, since that one is based on the old Latin creed of Rome, it didn't catch on among the Eastern churches, which used Greek. In addition to Roman Catholics, major Protestant leaders like Martin Luther and John Calvin accepted the Apostles' Creed and used it in their churches. This creed is still widely used by many evangelical Christians today.

Same-Saying with the Ancients

Does your church recite creeds? Perhaps you think they are the outdated musings of long-dead people, just obsolete words that don't have much use in modern churches. Or you might think they require rote repetition—never varying, never changing, and therefore boring.

But actually, a creed's lack of variance over the centuries is precisely its point. Creeds aren't supposed to have a new spin that changes with the times. They aren't intended to surprise you with clever wordings that some worship pastor rewrites each week. Instead, the point of a creed is to "same-say" the age-old truths of the Christian faith. Creeds declare what God has revealed in his Scriptures: the grand drama of creation, incarnation, crucifixion, resurrection, ascension, proclamation, and consummation.

Creeds also help you same-say the doctrines of the faith alongside your global brothers and sisters in Christ. When you recite a creed on Sunday, you can be confident that there are people around the world doing the same thing. Furthermore, the words you are speaking have been uttered by countless believers in the Christian past, men and women who were worshiping the same Savior as you. Creeds unite us around a common faith—across the miles and through the ages.

It really does matter what you say out loud. Regular verbal confession forms and shapes you. Let it be your delight that when you recite an ancient creed, you're same-saying what God's people have been confessing with their mouths for the last two thousand years. Surely these great truths will continue to ring from the lips of the redeemed in the eternal ages to come.

We have seen and testify that the Father has sent his Son
to be the Savior of the world. Whoever confesses that Jesus
is the Son of God, God abides in him, and he in God.

1 John 4:14-15

◆ 15 ◆

Christian Teachers
Construct the Christian World

We live in the so-called Information Age. Sometimes we forget how powerfully the mass media influences us. It used to be that we would be shaped by whatever media we chose to consume: the radio stations we dialed up, the TV channels we switched to, the movies we went to go see. Even the internet used to be a matter of whatever web pages we chose to browse. But now, with the advent of tracking technologies and social media, our digital diet is fed to us by powerful algorithms that know exactly who we are—and who Big Tech thinks we ought to be. It's scary to consider the power the media has to sculpt our minds and shape us as human beings.

Of course, the absence of mass media among ancient people didn't mean they weren't being influenced by powerful cultural forces. The ancients didn't have FaceCodex or InstaScroll, nor did they carry homing pigeons in their pockets to exchange swift messages back and forth. Even so, they were still being pressed into a unified worldview. Pagan mythology and religion, interlinked across the Roman Empire, played a formative role in that society. How could the early Christians resist this false narrative and create a godly counterculture? It was hard work, yet necessary. And one of the foremost ways they did it was through their Christian teachers.

In the ancient church, teaching was conveyed in two primary places. First, there was the formal instruction that took place when someone accepted Jesus as Lord and asked for baptism. This was (and still is) known as *catechesis*, which comes from the Greek word meaning "teaching by word of mouth." The second kind of ongoing teaching came through the preaching of the Word that happened in the weekly assemblies. Together, these two kinds of teaching forged a Christian worldview among people who had formerly been captivated by empty myths.

Counting the Cost

The early Christians demanded a rigorous process of pre-baptismal instruction. One reason for their slow and meticulous approach was the massive worldview shift that happened when someone left paganism and embarked upon the Christian journey. It took a lot of effort to deconstruct a heathen mindset and replace it with a truly Christian outlook. Baptism was the outward manifestation of a profound mental and spiritual washing.

Yet there was another reason for lengthy catechesis. At least in the first three centuries of church history, a believer in Jesus might experience hostility, rejection, or maybe even martyrdom. The ancients didn't want their baptized believers—the full members of the Christian community who had publicly professed their allegiance to a new Lord—to fall by the wayside when the fires of persecution assailed them. If someone was going to undergo the sober and serious rite of Christian initiation, they had better know what they were getting themselves into.

Jesus himself emphasized this mental preparation. When the disciples said they wanted to share in his coming glory, he replied with a challenge: "Can you drink the cup I drink or be baptized with the baptism I am baptized with?" (Mark 10:38). What was this "baptism" that Jesus was facing? It was the long, hard road to the cross (Luke 12:50). For the early Christians, the baptism of water could quickly turn into the baptism of blood. They had to be prepared for this fearsome possibility by a period of extensive catechesis. That way, they could count the cost before they took the plunge.

The People of the White Robes

The Christians who had put themselves forward for baptismal catechesis were called *catechumens*, and their teacher was known as their *catechist*. The relationship between a catechist and his catechumens shouldn't be viewed like a university professor who lectures in an academic hall, goes home, and doesn't see the students again until the next class period. In one sense, the analogy works because catechists did lecture on doctrine in the house churches, or later, in purpose-built rooms next to the baptistery. But we need to envision a much warmer relationship than what most academic lecturers would have with their pupils. The catechist was a spiritual mentor who walked closely with his students through the spiritual fires they were facing—including the fires of possible martyrdom. Two examples will illustrate what I mean.

One of the most beautiful relationships in the annals of church history was the one shared by the martyr Perpetua and her catechist Saturus.[1] Twenty-two-year-old Perpetua was a newly baptized Christian when she was arrested for her faith. In the terrible confines of the dungeon, she received a prophetic vision to tell her whether to expect a release or death. She saw a ladder stretching to heaven, with a fierce dragon at its base and dangerous blades along its length. In this scary moment, Saturus provided the needed courage. Boldly, he climbed the ladder, then turned around and beckoned to his sister in the faith. "I'm waiting for you, Perpetua," he said. "Just make sure the dragon doesn't bite you."

"He will not hurt me in the name of Jesus Christ," Perpetua replied. Then this brave heroine trod on the dragon's head (Genesis 3:15; Psalm 91:13; Luke 10:17-20) and ascended the ladder. At the top, she met an old man with white hair, milking his sheep. He was surrounded by white-robed saints. The shepherd welcomed her to his heavenly garden and gave her curds of indescribable sweetness. Then Perpetua woke up, knowing there would be a martyrdom. From then on, she thought no more of earth and set her eyes on things above.

If you have read chapter 2 of this book, you know the outcome

---

1. For the whole story, see Litfin, *Martyr Stories*, chapter 8.

of this story, but let's revisit it here. On the day the martyrs would be cast to the wild beasts in the amphitheater, they were supposed to be dressed in the garments of the pagan priesthood. But when they protested, they were allowed to wear instead the white robes of their recent baptism. Inside the arena, Saturus was gashed by a leopard and washed in blood. Perpetua was trampled by a mad cow. In this wounded and delirious state, the martyrs were rounded up for the final kill. The ancient editor of the story tells us:

> A little later Saturus was tossed unconscious with the other martyrs in the room where the throats of the dying are normally slit. But the mob demanded the martyrs be brought into the open…The martyrs willingly stood up and went over to the place the people wanted. But first they kissed one another, and in so doing they consummated their martyrdom with the kiss of peace. Each of them remained completely still and took the sword silently, especially Saturus. Just as he was the first to ascend the ladder in the dream, so he was the first to give up his spirit. Once again, he was waiting for Perpetua![2]

Saturus the teacher led the way to death for Perpetua and his other faithful students. Now those believers are once again feasting on the sweet curds of the Good Shepherd. May the day soon come when we join them at the wedding supper of the Lamb!

This stirring account of the love between a catechist and his disciples is matched by a story about Saint Patrick, the famous missionary to the Irish people. (Yes, he was an actual figure from the early church, despite all the crazy legends about shamrocks, snakes, and suds that eventually grew up around him.) The real Patrick was a British teenager who was captured in a slave raid and trafficked to Ireland, where he was forced to work as a shepherd on that cold and rainy island for many years. During that trial, he rededicated his life to Jesus, the only comforter of his lonely soul.

---

2. *Martyr Stories*, 108.

After Patrick escaped Ireland and returned to his British homeland, he experienced a missionary call to the very people who had victimized him. Recrossing the Irish Sea, he evangelized the locals with great success. Thousands of heathen Irish people converted to Christ due to his ministry.

A joyous day came when Patrick had just baptized a flock of new converts. Whenever early Christians were baptized, they were given white robes, which they wore for about a week afterward (Galatians 3:27). But in the midst of this happy celebration, tragedy struck. A band of cruel raiders hit the unsuspecting village where Patrick's converts lived. These human traffickers slaughtered many Christians and carried away the boys and girls to a terrible fate of brutal mistreatment and sex slavery. Furious, Patrick wrote a letter to the king who had ordered the raid, a tyrant named Coroticus. Although Patrick demanded the captives be returned, the wicked king refused. And so, with the love of a teacher for his newly baptized converts, Patrick lamented,

> O most beautiful brothers and sons whom I have begotten in Christ, countless in number! What can I do for you now? I'm not able to do anything...and so I mourn for you—I mourn, my dear ones! Yet at the same time, I rejoice within myself. Not for nothing have I labored, nor has my exile been in vain. And if this crime, so horrible, so unspeakable, had to happen, thanks be to God that you have departed from this world to paradise as baptized believers. I can see you clearly: you have begun to journey where night shall be no more, nor shall there be any mourning or death...Then you will reign with the apostles and prophets and martyrs; you will take possession of the realms of eternity![3]

Just as with Saturus and Perpetua, so we see here the lovely bond of affection and mentorship that existed between an ancient catechist and his white-robed spiritual offspring.

---

3. Bryan Litfin, *Getting to Know the Church Fathers* (2nd. ed., 2016) 273.

Preach the Word

After new Christians were catechized and baptized, their ongoing instruction came from their bishop, who preached the weekly sermons. Though the ancient church had many great preachers, two stand out from the rest.

The first was John Chrysostom, whose nickname means "golden-mouthed" because he was such an eloquent preacher. John was trained in the ancient art of rhetoric, whose three goals were to teach, to please, and to persuade. With fire in his eyes and zeal in his heart, John did each of these things for his congregations at Antioch and then Constantinople. His golden sermons instructed his flock in Christian doctrine, pleased them with vivid imagery, and persuaded them to exchange the allurements of their culture for the upward call of the gospel. So great was John's oratory that when his secular teacher was asked who should succeed him, he ruefully replied, "It should have been John, had not the Christians stolen him from us."[4] But we can be glad they did, for John's sermons powerfully shaped his generation of Christian believers.

The second noteworthy preacher of the ancient church was Augustine of Hippo, whose greatness was due not only to his eloquence but the profundity of his theology. Like all ancient preachers, Augustine would sit in his chair called a *cathedra* with the Scriptures on his lap while the congregation stood in the church hall and listened. On summer days, he dripped with sweat. Other times, his voice was hoarse. Augustine was known to chastise his flock for being distracted, or too anxious to get home for Sunday lunch, or for liking the clown shows in the circus more than his sermons. And if the lector accidentally read the wrong passage of Scripture to the congregation, Augustine would compose a new sermon on the spot and preach it instead! From his chair in the little church at Hippo, the mighty bishop would cajole and amuse, thunder and exhort, instruct and advise. In this way, he turned the affections of the people away from the city of man toward the eternal city of God.

---

4. Sozomen, *Church History* 8.2.

Over the course of his ministry, Augustine delivered around eight thousand sermons, of which approximately 560 survive in transcripts that were copied down by stenographers. His book *On Christian Teaching* tells us his goal in preaching: to rightly handle the divine Scriptures; defend the true faith and oppose error; teach the good and unteach evil; win over those who are hostile; stir up the slackers; and inform the ignorant of what's happening now and what is likely to come in the future.[5] This is wonderful advice, not only for the early Christians but for teachers of every generation!

On one occasion, Augustine was preaching powerfully on Galatians 6:14. When he proclaimed the words, "May I never boast except in the cross of our Lord Jesus Christ, through which the world has been crucified to me, and I to the world," the entire congregation burst into cheers for their beloved Savior. These ancient people, who had been steeped in pagan mythology and the worship of the gods, were now so moved by Jesus that they couldn't contain the exuberance of their newfound joy. In this image, we discover a truth that preachers like Augustine and John Chrysostom knew well, along with catechists like Saturus and Patrick: That when the Christian mind has been formed by Spirit-led teachers, the transformation is total and everlasting.

> *Go and make disciples of all nations, baptizing them in the name of the Father and of the Son and of the Holy Spirit, and teaching them to obey everything I have commanded you.*
>
> MATTHEW 28:19-20

---

5. *On Christian Teaching* 4.4.6. This writing is also commonly known as *On Christian Doctrine*.

16

Baptism Moves You
into a Whole New World

The one ritual practiced by virtually all types of Christians—from every denomination, whether high church, low church, or anything in between—is baptism. Jesus himself was baptized (Matthew 3:16). The command to continue doing it was part of the final instructions he gave to his followers when he was leaving them (Matthew 28:19). Then, after he had ascended to heaven, we see the early Christians doing a lot of baptizing in the book of Acts. For these reasons, baptism is a universal Christian practice. Everybody agrees it should be done.

But what, exactly, does it mean? I think it would be safe to say that the ancient Christians didn't have a single, monolithic view of baptism. Beliefs varied among individual writers at different times. Yet there was one thing they agreed about: Its decisive and immediate transfer from one kingdom to another. Baptism moved you out of Satan's domain and into God's. This is the important theme that I'd like to put on display in this chapter as I depict the baptismal practices of the ancient church.

To accomplish this, allow me to do a bit of imagination with you. I will tell you the story of two fictional people: Marius, a shoemaker in Rome, and his wife, Lucilla. Let us imagine that around AD 200, this couple heard the gospel and received it like good seed falling onto ready soil. Previously, Marius had a special affinity for Mercury, the god of trade, as well as the ancestral spirits of his household shrine. For her part, Lucilla had been fond of the mother goddess Isis, imported from Egypt. Now, however, they have rejected those pagan deities and have indicated they wish to be baptized in the name of the Lord Jesus Christ. What would their experiences have been like?

Fortunately their baptismal process isn't hard to reconstruct. Although these two characters are made up, the story that follows is based on an actual, historical document from this exact time. Known as the *Apostolic Tradition*, it is one of several church manuals that describe the different things pastors are supposed to do for their congregations. This text gives us a real-world look into many aspects of the Christian life in ancient times, including baptism. The following narrative is taken directly from the ideas and sequence found in the *Apostolic Tradition*.

The Baptism of Marius and Lucilla

The married couple is first brought before the teachers of the church, where they are questioned about their faith and morals. The sponsor who brought them vouches for their character. Marius and Lucilla are taught to be sexually faithful to each other—a surprising demand because men commonly have extramarital liaisons—yet they accept the new requirement. Since it is apparent that they haven't picked up any demons during their days of pagan worship, no exorcism is required just yet. And since Marius's occupation is selling shoes, the couple is allowed to proceed toward baptism. If he had been a pimp, a sculptor of idols, a gladiator, an executioner, a magician, or a fortune-teller, he would have been required to give up those professions, which are incompatible with the Christian faith.

A formal catechesis of up to three years now takes place, during which Marius and Lucilla learn the doctrines of Christianity and allow their lives to be examined for works of charity and moral purity. At last, after much instruction and prayer, the Sunday of baptism approaches. On Thursday Marius and Lucilla take a bath, and on Friday they fast.

On Saturday they gather with the other baptismal candidates and receive an exorcism from the bishop. Then the bishop breathes on them and makes a cross on their foreheads, ears, and nostrils.[1] Marius and Lucilla, along with their Christian friends, spend the whole night in a prayer vigil at the church.

At sunrise on Sunday morning, the candidates approach a household bathing facility through which water is flowing. In the golden light of dawn, everyone removes their clothes.[2] Lucilla also sets aside her jewelry and unties her hair, leaving no knots for demons to cling to; for knots are part of occult magic. The children are baptized first, with the parents speaking for those who are too young to speak for themselves. Then Marius is baptized with the men, and afterward Lucilla with the women.

The bishop has prepared two kinds of oil. He oversees the proceedings as a presbyter anoints the Christians with the oil of exorcism, assisted by deacons. Marius is told to say, "I renounce thee, Satan, and all thy servants and works." Then the presbyter replies, "Let every evil spirit depart from you." Standing naked in the water, Marius is asked whether he believes the three articles of the creed. He is asked first about the Father, then about the Son, then about the Holy Spirit in the church. Each time that Marius is interrogated with the words of the creed, he replies, *Credo*—"I believe." Upon his profession of faith, he goes down into the water three times and comes up into newness of life.

Marius now emerges from the water after crossing the font like the Israelites passing through the Red Sea as they left Egypt. The presbyter anoints his head with the second oil, the oil of thanksgiving. Marius receives a new white robe, which he will wear for the coming week. After Marius and Lucilla dry off and re-dress, they joyfully proceed

---

1. In other accounts of ancient baptism, the bishop often says at this point, "*Ephphatha!*" ("Be opened!"; Mark 7:34).

2. The meaning behind this practice is obvious—to leave behind everything from the old life—but exactly how modesty was preserved is difficult for us to understand. Some historians think the genders were baptized separately, with the opposite one absent as they took turns. Or perhaps a screen was put up to hide the opposite sex from view. On the other hand, it may be that nude baptism was practiced in the sight of all, and purity of heart was expected from true believers despite the visual temptation.

with their friends to a room where the elements of communion have been prepared.

In the church hall, the bishop lays his hands on each of the baptized believers. He prays over them and anoints them again with the oil of thanksgiving, blessing them in the name of the Father, Son, and Holy Spirit. After some final prayers are said, the washed and sanctified believers exchange the kiss of peace.

At last, this Christian couple is allowed to partake of the holy elements with their baptized friends. For the first time ever, they witness the bishop consecrating the bread and wine, which are explained to be an "image" and "likeness" of Christ's body and blood. Marius and Lucilla also receive a mixture of milk and honey. Through their Savior, they have reached God's promised land. They drink some water too, so that their inner souls may have the same baptism as the outer body. Three times, the recipients partake of each substance in the name of the Trinity. When communion is finished, all the Christians are dismissed with an exhortation to do good works, please God, live honorably, be devoted to the church, and obey the things they were taught as they grow in holiness of life.

A Whole New World

The story of Marius and Lucilla gives us a vivid picture of baptism as it was understood around the beginning of the third century. We must keep in mind that the theological arguments of the Protestant Reformation were still many centuries in the future. Baptism wasn't *either* a saving work *or* a symbol of inner faith, but both at the same time. The ancients assumed that inward faith and outward obedience to Christ's command must go together. "Whoever believes and is baptized will be saved, but whoever does not believe will be condemned," Jesus had told his disciples (Mark 16:16). Could it be any clearer? If you believed in Jesus, you were baptized into him. It really was as simple as that.

But as we consider the simplicity of this ancient ritual, let us not miss some of the significant details in what we just observed. As I noted above, early Christian baptism was understood to transfer the recipient from the kingdom of Satan (and of his demonic or human servants) to the kingdom of God. Marius and Lucilla were being liberated from false lords such as Caesar or the gods. They were escaping tyranny to find true freedom in the Lord of lords who reigns on high.

This is why exorcism was such an important part of the baptismal rite. The Bible teaches that the deities the pagans worshiped as "gods" were actually demonic spirits who held people in bondage (1 Corinthians 10:20). For converts who were steeped in that sort of religion, baptism was a cleansing from evil spirits. Today, many global Christians from places where magic or witchcraft is prevalent know this very well. Baptism means escaping from the occult. So too, a big part of early Christian baptism was renouncing Satan, leaving his chains behind, and entering into the freedom of Christ the Victor.

Another important idea—and certainly a related one—was the journey motif, in which Christians left an oppressive kingdom and entered a joyous new land. Therefore, the exodus of the Israelites provided important baptismal imagery for the ancient church. In Egypt, the people of God were enslaved by wicked Pharaoh. But after the blood of the Passover lamb was shed, they were led out by a mighty deliverer into a wilderness. They left everything behind: All the trappings of an alien society now in their past. In the wilderness, the Israelites were metaphorically naked—helpless before God and utterly dependent on him.

And yet, in the midst of their difficult trials, Christ Jesus was the Rock who provided living water, an image which is beautifully celebrated across the whole arc of Scripture (Exodus 17:6; Numbers 20:11; Psalm 78:15, 105:41; John 4:10-13, 7:37-38; 1 Corinthians 10:4). The wandering Israelites passed through the water of the Red Sea before triumphantly arriving in a land flowing with milk and honey, a land of abundance—the promised land of God.

A Watery Grave

In addition to these themes of exorcism and kingdom transference, let us not miss, with our modern perspective, the significance of baptism by immersion. The ancient Christians believed that you had to go underwater, either by having water poured over you or, preferably, by plunging beneath the water's surface in a pool. Let's consider the important symbolism in this.

Today we think of the ocean as happy and safe, like a pleasant place to go boating or a beautiful beach where we can play in the waves. The sea is a destination for relaxing holidays. But in the ancient mindset, the sea was a deadly terror where it was risky to go and from which you might not return. Monsters lurked in such a dreadful abyss ("Leviathan" according to Psalm 74:13-14). The ocean was a place of permanent death—except in one case when the unfathomable deep was not allowed to prevail over the life of a certain man. Which man?

In the Italian town of Aquileia, there is a beautiful eleventh-century basilica whose floor has been removed to reveal the stunning mosaics that adorned the floor of a much earlier building. This original church goes back to the fourth century, the work of an industrious bishop named Theodore. There were two side-by-side halls in that church: one for the Sunday communion service and one for baptisms. Although the mosaic floors of both halls are amazing, the one from the baptismal hall particularly catches the eye.

Since Aquileia is a coastal town, the mosaics depict scenes of fishermen and many exotic sea creatures. Yet interspersed among these images is the story of Jonah. In one scene, naked Jonah is swallowed by a coiled sea serpent. In the second, he is bursting from the monster's belly, diving onto a platform with his arms extended. And in the final scene, Jonah reclines upon the platform beneath an arbor of vines, at rest under the shade of God.

What does this mean? Death...resurrection...paradise. Is this not the story of the Christian life? And is this not what is depicted by baptism when the waters of the abyss close over your head, when you are entombed in the deep, when you descend into the place of deadly monsters? But where, o death, is your sting? The grave cannot hold you; Satan cannot have you; sin cannot defeat you. Not if you are in Christ! And so, like Jonah of old, you burst from the belly of the beast and find yourself received into the garden of the Lord. That, in short, is what early Christian baptism was all about—and what baptism in the name of Jesus still offers today.

As you reflect on these various images, can you hear the church fathers calling to you across the ages, trying to help you understand the deep things of God? Do you hear them asking, "Brothers and sisters of the future, isn't this the journey you experienced at your salvation as well? Weren't you, like us, delivered from Satan's darkness into a kingdom of light? Didn't you also come bursting from the watery grave into glorious new life?" Listen well to the ancients. They have important lessons to teach us about the sacred nature of Christian baptism.

Don't you know that all of us who were baptized into
Christ Jesus were baptized into his death?
We were therefore buried with him through baptism into death
in order that, just as Christ was raised from the dead
through the glory of the Father,
we too may live a new life.

ROMANS 6:3-4

17

There's a Lot More
Flavor to the Lord's Supper
Than You Might Think

I n the previous chapter, I said that the one ritual that all Christians practice is water baptism. But I spoke too soon. There's another Christian observance that's nearly universal among groups that call themselves Christians: holy communion. The two elements of this ritual are bread (leavened or unleavened) and juice from grapes (fermented or unfermented). These elements point to the body and blood of Jesus upon the cross. Beyond this, there is little agreement about what communion actually means.

This has always been the case. The reason there's so much disagreement about the theological meaning of communion is that numerous overlapping themes coexisted in the early church. And I don't just mean among the Christians who lived after the age of the apostles. Even among the New Testament writers themselves—and thus within its pages—there were multiple layers of meaning attached to communion.

There's nothing wrong with that. Variety is a good thing. It's like a delicious soup. Who would want to eat a soup that consists only of boiled carrots? Yuck! The most delicious soups have lots of ingredients, flavors, and seasonings. They all converge to make a great taste. So too, one of the most central practices of Christianity—the Lord's Supper—is like a bubbling soup comprised of many different flavors that make it tasty. Our problem is, we've split into factions that focus on various "views" about communion. Some Christians choose to taste only the vegetables, some the meat, some the seasonings, and some the broth. But why not taste the whole theological soup when you come to the communion table?

In this chapter, I want to focus on how the ancient Christians understood the various aspects of communion. I will focus on five key ingredients that combine to form a delicious whole: remembrance, spiritual nourishment, charity, table fellowship, and a heavenly banquet. All these aspects were important for the early Christian view of the bread and the cup. Together, they can help us understand what we're doing on Sunday when we bring the wafer and wine[1] to our lips.

"Do This in Remembrance of Me."

When Jesus reclined with his disciples in the upper room as they celebrated their final Passover meal, he took bread and wine, distributed it, and said, "Do this in remembrance of me" (Luke 22:19-20; 1 Corinthians 11:24-25). The word *remembrance* comes from a verb that means "to remind, call to memory." Clearly, when we celebrate communion, we're supposed to let that broken piece of bread and the glistening red liquid remind us of Jesus' sacrifice upon the cross. In this way, as Paul says, we "proclaim the Lord's death until he comes" (1 Corinthians 11:26). Communion is a memorial of Christ's passion.

---

1. In the Bible, "wine" refers to a drink that was alcoholic, though it was normally diluted with water to make it less intoxicating. Nonalcoholic wine could only be consumed if somebody drank the juice right after pressing the grapes. Natural sugars and yeast in the air would start fermenting the juice immediately, so that after a short time, all wine had a low percentage of alcohol, at which point it would kill the yeast and stop the fermentation. Despite what you may have heard, there was no such thing in ancient times as permanently unfermented grape juice. The ancients didn't have the technology (or the incentive) to do that. In this chapter, *wine* will serve as a general term to describe the drink that is consumed in communion—though I recognize and affirm that many churches today (including mine) seek to honor God by not serving alcohol to the congregation.

What feelings are we likely to experience as we remember our Savior's death? One of them is certainly gratitude. For this reason, the ancient Christians thought of communion as a thank offering like those in the Old Testament for times when people felt grateful for God's gifts (Leviticus 7:12). This is where the term *Holy Eucharist* originates. The Bible uses the Greek verb *eucharisteō* when it tells us that Jesus "gave thanks" and broke the bread. Because of Jesus' example, the early Christians lifted up the bread and wine to thank God for his gracious salvation. Communion (or the Eucharist) was a remembrance of gratitude for Christ's saving sacrifice.

Yet it was more than just a thank offering. It also replaced the sin offerings of the Jewish Law because it commemorated the once-for-all death of the Passover lamb (John 1:29; 1 Corinthians 5:7; 1 Peter 1:19). One of the church fathers' favorite passages was Malachi 1:10-11, where the prophet contrasts the impure offerings that some Israelites were offering with the pure ones that God actually desires. Bishop Irenaeus of Lyon declared that "the former people shall indeed cease to make offerings. But in every place, [a new] sacrifice shall be offered to Him, a pure one; and [so] His name is glorified among the Gentiles."[2] Communion points back to the cross of Christ in the same way the Jewish sacrifices had previewed it for centuries. When we partake of the Lord's Supper, we are celebrating Christ's work with remembrance and thanksgiving.

"I Am the Bread of Life."

Alongside the idea of a memorial sacrifice was the idea of spiritual food and drink. The church fathers didn't try to figure out *how* the bread and wine nourished their souls, but they were sure it did. This was because Jesus, in a mysterious way, was present in the elements. Although theological discussions from a much later time attempted to define exactly what was going on here, the ancient Christians were content just to take Jesus at his word. When he held up a piece of bread, he

---

2. *Against Heresies* 4.17.5.

said, "This is my body." When he held up a cup, he said, "This is my blood of the covenant" (Matthew 26:26-28). *This is that.* Pretty simple.

Though Jesus was using symbolism here, he was also affirming the idea of communion as spiritual nourishment. That is why he could say, "Whoever eats my flesh and drinks my blood has eternal life, and I will raise them up at the last day. For my flesh is real food and my blood is real drink" (John 6:54-55). Obviously this wasn't literal cannibalism. It was, however, real feeding upon our Savior. Jesus promised that "the one who feeds on me will live because of me" (v. 57).

The ancient apologist Justin Martyr, who lived in the middle of the second century, gave us one of the clearest descriptions of what the ancient church believed about communion. Justin explained, "And this food is called among us 'the Eucharist'...Not as common bread nor common drink do we receive these things...We have been taught that the food which is 'eucharistized' by the prayer of Jesus' word, which nourishes our flesh and blood through this change, is the flesh and blood of the very Jesus who became incarnate."[3] Justin wasn't attempting to offer some strange theory about priestly transformation of bread and wine. He was simply taking the Lord at face value when he said "this is my body" and "this is my blood." Because Jesus was especially present with believers in communion, spiritual nourishment was available to them.

"Blemishes at Your Love Feasts."

A third important aspect of ancient communion was love. Christians were meant to share this meal as brothers and sisters who loved each other in the Lord. That is why the apostle Jude, who was Jesus' brother, grew angry when heretics started creeping into the Christian meals so they could stuff their faces. "These people are blemishes at your love feasts," Jude boldly declared, "eating with you without the slightest qualm—shepherds who feed only themselves" (Jude 1:12). The apostle Paul also criticized the selfishness of those who gorged themselves on

---

3. *First Apology* 66, translation mine.

their own food at the Lord's Supper or got drunk (1 Corinthians 11:20-22). Clearly, that wasn't an act of love!

We should notice here that the Lord's Supper wasn't a tiny wafer and an itty-bitty juice cup. These ancient people were eating actual meals—and this meant more than you might realize. When Jude described the "love feast," his Greek term was *agapē*, or sacrificial love. Even today, some Christians still celebrate an "agape," a potluck supper enjoyed as a time of harmonious fellowship and brotherly love. But for the ancient church, this meal was about more than just friendly relations over good food and drink. Consider that the Latin word for *agapē* was *caritas*, or "charity." This meal was about charity in every sense of the word: not just the emotion of love, but literal charity for the poor, whose bellies were often empty. One day a week, these impoverished Christians knew that their stomachs would cease growling and they'd have the same full feeling that the rich enjoyed.

Eventually, charitable giving in the ancient church began to be distributed in other ways, so the Sunday celebration of communion became separated from the original love feast. Even so, this practice of the earliest Christians reminds us that the true spirit of communion is love—a love backed up by concrete actions that take care of the needy.

"This Man Welcomes Sinners and Eats with Them."

One of Jesus' most startling practices was his willingness to eat at the tables of known sinners. In first-century Judaism, the tax collectors who collaborated with Rome were a hated bunch. Yet Jesus willingly ate meals with them, which at that time signified acceptance. When the Pharisees criticized such behavior that seemed unworthy of a rabbi, Jesus' response was, "I have not come to call the righteous, but sinners to repentance" (Luke 5:32). He was willing to cross strict social boundaries to show God's mercy and grace.

The early Christians continued this pattern. Their love feasts, as I mentioned above, were held in houses that mixed the wealthy and poor together. Many pagans mocked the Christians for being the dregs of society: indigent, unwashed, the outcasts of life. And indeed, many of them were. Yet some believers were wealthy and had beautiful homes. Imagine that at your next Thanksgiving feast, when all your family and friends are ready to sit down to a lovely banquet, the door swings open and five rough guys march in from the local homeless shelter. Their words are crude, they smell of body odor and stale urine, and they even struggle with mental illness. Yet you welcome them warmly and grant them equal standing as family members. If some unbelievers at your table saw this, they would surely marvel. This is what ancient communion was about: table fellowship that blew apart social boundaries and displayed the radical equality of the body of Christ (Galatians 3:28; Colossians 3:11).

"Blessed Are Those Who Are Invited to the Wedding Supper of the Lamb!"

The final aspect of ancient communion that I wish to highlight is its orientation toward a future heavenly banquet. All believers wait eagerly for what John described as the "wedding supper of the Lamb" (Revelation 19:9). For the early Christians, communion was a foretaste of that great eschatological feast. Jesus made this connection clear when he said that his cup of wine at the Last Supper was his last until God's kingdom would arrive: "I will not drink from this fruit of the vine from now on until that day when I drink it new with you in my Father's kingdom" (Matthew 26:29).

When the ancients partook of communion, they were displaying their unity with all Christians who had put their hope in the Lord's glorious return. Everyone awaited this common destiny, even if they weren't physically present for the ritual. To depict this truth, the deacons distributed a piece of the Eucharistic loaf and the blessed wine to those who couldn't meet in the church that Sunday. This fulfilled the words of 1 Corinthians 10:16-17, "Is not the cup of thanksgiving for which we give thanks a participation in the blood of Christ? And is not the bread that we break a participation in the body of Christ? Because there is one loaf, we, who are many, are one body, for we all share the one loaf."

The word *participation* in the verse above is normally translated in Latin as *communio*. To take communion is to experience a union that transcends not only physical distance but also the passing of time. When we share this meal together, we do it within the context of what the Apostles' Creed calls "the communion of the saints"—the fellowship of all those who have ever loved Jesus. The Christians who went before us aren't gone forever, since "God will bring with Jesus those who have fallen asleep in him" (1 Thessalonians 4:14). Communion points to a glorious future when the Lamb who was slain becomes a rider on a white horse who conquers Satan, sin, and even death itself.

In light of all this, you might be wondering why your communion is so bland, why your cracker and juice are so plain and tasteless. Are you missing something? Perhaps communion was meant to be more flavorful? Of course, I'm not suggesting that your literal taste buds should explode with flavor the next time you partake of the Lord's Supper. Your tongue should taste the same thing as always. Yet having received these insights from the ancient church, perhaps the next time you celebrate communion, your soul will taste so much more.

Very truly I tell you, unless you eat the flesh of the Son
of Man and drink his blood, you have no life in you.

JOHN 6:53

18

Sin Is a Sickness, but Grace Is Just What the Doctor Ordered

The starting point of the Christian gospel isn't good news, but bad: "You are a sinner." The gospel is only good news if there's a dilemma that needs to be remedied. Christianity has always taught that in addition to the moral sins we choose to commit, all people have a sinful disposition that was passed down to us from Adam. This doctrine is based not only on the story of Adam and Eve in Genesis 3, but on what the apostle Paul teaches in Romans 5:12, namely, that "sin entered the world through one man [Adam], and death through sin, and in this way death came to all people, because all sinned."

We humans need salvation because we have received the curse of sin from Adam. This burden upon our souls has resulted in universal sinful behavior—by you, me, and everyone who has ever lived (except Jesus). But the theological question remains: What *exactly* did Adam send our way? In other words, by what mechanism or mode of transmission is our sinfulness related to his? On this point, the church has not always said the same thing. Yet once again, the ancient Christians offer some useful insights for us.

Views of Adamic Sin

Perhaps one way to understand the early Christians' teaching about sin (known in theological parlance as "hamartiology") is to consider other historical views that were not as prominent among the ancients. I say "not as prominent" because you can certainly find these themes in some ancient writers. However, these views weren't the main way the church fathers framed these issues. Even so, they help to clarify what the ancient church actually did teach with respect to these topics.

One model of sin's transmission from Adam focuses on the idea of *seeds*. Unfortunately, this view is based on an incorrect understanding of human reproduction. Ancient people thought that men had tiny seeds of their future descendants within them (the Latin word for seed is *semen*), while the female uterus was like the soil in which the seed was planted. But if a man's body contained the seed of his future prog- eny as a kind of miniature human being, doesn't that mean the seed must have its own seed within it—in even tinier form? If you keep on going with this idea, you arrive at the conclusion that the seeds of everybody must have been "seminally present" within Adam, the fore- father of all human beings. So, in a sense, we were all "there" when Adam sinned. We got contaminated—body and soul—by his rebel- lious action. Through corrupted human reproduction, we've been sin- ners ever since. The seminal or seed idea was held by church fathers in the Western, Latin speaking part of the Roman Empire—especially Tertullian and Augustine.

A second model of Adamic hamartiology emphasizes the idea of *representation*. Although the ancient church fathers did think of Adam as our representative, this view was more robustly developed in the time of the Reformation, in the context of what is called "covenant theology." The idea here is that God named Adam as our representa- tive. This one man was placed at the head of a covenant that God made with the human race. Since the word *federal* refers to a covenant, this is sometimes called the "federal headship" view. When Adam sinned, all those he represented were plunged into sin as well. It's like an ambassa- dor declaring war against a foreign country. Once he or she takes this step, all the citizens of the nation are at war with that enemy. The action of the representative affects all those who are represented. While the church fathers did regard Adam as our representative, they didn't really hold this covenantal view.

A third view that was accepted by quite a few people in ancient times is now considered a heresy. The leader of this outlook was a popular and persuasive monk from Britain named Pelagius (active in the early 400s). The Pelagian view says that, in fact, no sin was transmitted to us from Adam. We are mistaken if we think he actually affected us. All he did was leave us a very bad example, and we've been stupidly following it ever since. However, we can choose to do differently if we wish. We have total free will, uncompromised by any inherited sin. When we choose the right things, God gives us more grace to help us further along. If we keep making the right decisions, we will earn our way to heaven. Since this view taught earned salvation in which grace only offered a boost for what we ourselves had started, it caught the attention of many theologians who considered it entirely unbiblical. And the foremost opponent of the Pelagian heresy was the great African bishop, Augustine of Hippo.

Augustine, the Teacher of Grace

The most impactful book written by any of the church fathers is Augustine's prayerful autobiography, the *Confessions*. The only book (outside the Bible) that might tie it for the top spot is his huge tome, *City of God*. Any other book from the ancient church would be below these two in terms of lasting impact on church history. In the *Confessions*, Augustine wrote a single sentence that gave Pelagius—to borrow an idiom from my Southern roots—a bee in his bonnet. Pelagius hated this statement and spent his whole career trying to refute it.

What was this offending sentence that bothered Pelagius so much? Augustine had written to God, "Command what you will, and grant what you command." (He actually wrote the clauses in the opposite order, but it makes more sense to express it in English like this.) Augustine was saying, "Lord, you can make any law or command that you want. But then you must give us the grace to be able to follow your rules, for we are lost and helpless sinners." The great bishop of Hippo was affirming that we have no innate ability to turn toward God or do his will. We are totally fallen in Adam. The grace to begin the Christian life has to be granted to us by God. In other words, the initiative for salvation doesn't begin with our own free will, which is far too corrupted for that. The first move has to come from God. Only then can we begin to walk more strongly in the Christian faith, always relying on God's gracious help to uphold us.

This Augustinian teaching is known as the doctrine of original sin. Although earlier Christian writers had spoken about the harmful effects of sin that had been passed to us from Adam, no one had yet articulated the precise contours of this doctrine. It says that we are all sinful in our inclinations and incapable of turning toward God apart from grace. The strongest form of it includes the idea of inheriting Adam's actual guilt, though not every ancient theologian believed that.

Yet eventually, everyone agreed that Pelagius's view had to be condemned. Adam's sin did, indeed, plunge the human race into sin. Although exactly *how* it happened wasn't clear—that's the subject of this chapter—the fact of universal human sinfulness became a fixed Christian doctrine at this moment of church history. Later generations would debate how closely they would hold to Augustine's precise views, but no one believed anymore in the raw works salvation that Pelagius and his associates had taught.

Is the Christian doctrine of original sin a pessimistic view that puts a rain cloud over the human race? Is it a sour and negative outlook that views people as evil fiends who are gross and malicious? While history has surely had its share of fiends—and the fiend within each of us is never far away—this doctrine actually emphasizes the love of God and his abundant grace. Although Augustine insisted, "It is not possible not to sin," he also celebrated divine grace so much that he came to be known in church history as the Teacher of Grace. The radiant splendor of God's goodness to us in Christ can be seen all the more clearly against the darkness of our sin. Augustine, who had lived a profligate life before his dramatic conversion in a Milanese garden, knew this very well. If you ever want to read the story of God's grace in the life of a redeemed sinner, Augustine's *Confessions* is a great place to start.

Although Augustine's view of humanity's total sinfulness and God's abundant grace marked an important milestone in church history, his "seed" view of sin's transmission leaves a lot to be desired. Even if we ignore its inaccurate view of human reproduction and just focus on our direct lineage from Adam as the mechanism for transmitting sin, it still leaves us in a strange place. Is sin somehow "attached" to a man's sperm? Is it some kind of genetic defect that gets passed to us in a mutation of our spiritual chromosomes? Is sexual intercourse defiled because it spawns new sin whenever a baby is conceived? I have to admit, these problems make me want to look for a different way to think about sin. So if we avoid the seed view, what else is there? I think the outlook of the Eastern church fathers works the best and is the most biblical approach.

The Eastern View: Sin as Sickness

One of the most common ways that the ancient Christians spoke about sin, especially (though by no means exclusively) among the Greek-speaking fathers in the East, was as a sickness, a disease, or a corruption. A related idea was a wound, a kind of death blow inflicted on humanity that eventually kills us all. Although the ancients didn't know about germs and bacteria, they certainly understood that a wound could get infected and devastate the entire body. They could see what happened when a terrible cancer overtook someone. They knew that a plague could enter a city and spread to everyone. Sin was like that: A virus that got a foothold and ran rampant until it killed the whole organism. For the human race, Adam was the gash that let in the germ of sin that destroyed us.

One of the most important Eastern fathers who discussed sin and its effects was Athanasius, a deacon and later the bishop of Alexandria in Egypt. He wrote a book that discussed why Jesus became incarnate, so of course, he had to address the topic of sin. Athanasius described it as a corruption, a disorder of the human self. Just as sickness ravages a person until they waste away to nothing, so Athanasius believed that unsaved people are falling into nonexistence. Sinners are in a process of becoming undone. Their very constitution is falling apart like a person in total organ failure. Indeed, sinners are the walking dead, mere zombies who can stagger around but who are actually becoming more sub-human by the moment. Corruption…ruin…destruction…dissolution—these things have taken hold of everyone. Into this terrible human dilemma, the God-Man came with a solution—but our exploration of that divine intervention must be reserved for the next chapter.

This disease or corruption view of sin fits nicely with what Paul describes in Romans 5:12. The apostle declares that "through one man sin entered into the world, and death through sin, and so death spread to all men, because all sinned" (NASB). Notice the verbs Paul uses here: *entered* and *spread*. He depicts sin as a harmful force that invades the world through an opening, allowing death to follow in its wake and spread among everyone. We all sin—why? Because sin and death entered the world through Adam, subjugating the human race and destroying its original, Edenic purity. This same concept can be found in the Old Testament purity laws that address skin diseases, mildew, decay, or even leaven in bread. Why did God care to make laws about such seemingly trivial things? Because they pictured the creeping and corrupting power of sin, an insidious force that can overtake something good and ruin it forever.

Although the ancients had various ways of speaking about sin, the disease/corruption model best helps us understand how secretive yet devastating sin can be. The cancer of sin that grew from Adam's original tumor requires the intervention of the Great Physician. Along with this important concept, we also learn from Augustine how total and complete our bondage to sin really is. There is no innocence left in us, no spark of goodness with which we can approach God. He, and he alone, must come to us with the gift of salvation. Yet once God kindles his divine flame in our hearts, it blazes into a bonfire of holy love. This is what the gospel of Jesus Christ offers to us. And it is to the ancient view of God's glorious salvation that we will turn in the next chapter.

> *Praise the LORD, my soul, and forget not all his benefits—who forgives all your sins and heals all your diseases, who redeems your life from the pit and crowns you with love and compassion.*
>
> PSALM 103:2-4

19

Mystical Union with God Wasn't Invented by "Eastern Religions," but by Jesus

What if I told you my religious faith is about helping humans achieve spiritual oneness with the divine? And then I called it a mystical experience that can't be fully expressed in words? Would you think I was a Buddhist? A New Ager? A practitioner of yoga, occultism, or Hare Krishna? Would you think I was a follower of Eastern religions who needed to hear the true gospel?

What if told you this *is* the true gospel?

Though you may not have heard the gospel expressed this way, mystical union with God really is the essence of Christianity. Let me show you what I mean.

The Mysterious Christian Faith

As I make my case for mystical union with God by drawing from the wisdom of the ancients, let's first tackle the "mystical" part. This word comes straight from the Greek, *mystikos*, and it's part of a cluster of words that all begin with *myst-*. These words designated something "mysterious," especially the teachings of the ancient sects known as mystery religions. Unlike the Greco-Roman paganism that had prominent temples on the public squares, the mystery religions were private and secretive. Another distinctive of such religions was that only a tiny sliver of the population would choose to join them. While the whole citizenry was automatically part of the public worship of the gods, only a few people would join the mystery religions. And when they did, they went through a secret rite of initiation.

Early Christianity was a mystery religion. Now, obviously, its belief system and its God were utterly different from the rest. The biblical God is a far cry from the cult worship of the Egyptian goddess Isis or the Greek god of wine, Dionysius. Even the mystery religion that came closest to looking like Christianity—Mithraism, which had a bloodshedding and dying-and-rising deity—was still different in fundamental ways from the ancient church. Christianity is unique in its worship of the one, true God—Father, Son, and Holy Spirit.

Nevertheless, Christianity was structured just like a mystery religion during the first three centuries of church history. It offered a more personal connection to the divine world than the public temples. Only a small percentage of people converted to this faith. When they did, they were baptized as a special rite of initiation and formed a tight-knit community. The early Christians didn't have grand public buildings (at least not at first). They met privately—indeed, secretly. Outsiders who hadn't yet left their pagan ways weren't allowed to partake of, or even see, the Lord's Supper. It was a holy ceremony reserved for the body of Christ. Only when someone had left the demons could they come to Christ's table.

The concept of "mystery" is widespread in biblical Christianity. The Greek word *mystērion* appears numerous times in the pages of Scripture. Jesus himself made this an important term when he explained to his disciples how his parables worked: "To you it has been granted to know the mysteries of the kingdom of God, but to the rest it is in parables" (Luke 8:10 NASB; see also Matthew 13:11; Mark 4:11). The apostle Paul also made great use of the mystery idea. In 1 Corinthians 2:7, he says, "we declare God's wisdom, a mystery that has been hidden and that God destined for our glory before time began." The idea of

Christianity as a long-hidden mystery that is now being revealed to God's people can be found everywhere in Paul's writings.

For the ancient church fathers, *mystikos* became a common word to explain the secret things of God that they practiced—the things that weren't revealed to everyone, certainly not to the pagans who scorned and mocked Christianity. Beyond their secret practices, the church fathers also believed that secret truths lay hidden within their Scriptures. To be mystical, then, is to preserve the mystery of what God is up to in his church. You can't always explain God's ways of working—not to outsiders, nor at times even to insiders. This is because the very nature of being mysterious is to defy precise verbal definitions. And that is who God is—a God whose ways are infinitely higher than ours (Isaiah 55:8-9).

The ancients were okay with mystery, but are we? Can we relinquish our desire to put everything into words, to capture truth in a verbal dragnet and define it to death? Are we willing to just sit back and live humbly in the mysteriousness of God? The church fathers didn't share our modern urge to reduce everything to words and formulas. They were fine just knowing that God was doing something incredible, without feeling the need to write a scientific treatise on exactly what was happening. If you are in that place too, keep reading. It's time to examine the second part of the term *mystical union*.

Recapitulating the Christian Story

The Christian gospel offers humans a union with God that we once possessed, but lost in tragic fashion. Humanity originally had perfect communion with God in the garden of Eden. But that fellowship was shattered when our forefather Adam opened the floodgates of evil. In the previous chapter, we saw that sin could be pictured as a corruption, a devastating disease that undoes us and sends us hurtling into oblivion. Everything that was once right and good, when God walked beside his creatures in the cool of the day, came unraveled when the serpent uncoiled his wily words. Now what are we supposed to do?

One of the first Christians to think systematically about the doctrine of salvation was Irenaeus of Lyon. His salvation theory (as we explored in chapter 12) is known by the Latin term *recapitulatio* or the Greek word *anakephalaiōsis*, both of which mean exactly the same thing: To reorganize something that has gotten disordered back under its proper headings.

Allow me to illustrate what this means. In my other life as a writer, I am a novelist. I can imagine a situation—what a horror!—in which my only manuscript of a novel has gotten corrupted in my computer. Somehow, all the chapters, scenes, and words have become so mixed up that the text is now meaningless. What must be done?

This big mess needs a "recapitulation"—a complete re-heading or re-chaptering (*capitalis* refers to a head or chapter). That is what Jesus Christ did for us, according to Irenaeus. At the incarnation, he entered our world and began to fix the mess that Adam started long ago, and which everyone has been making worse ever since. Jesus achieved what Adam could not: He perfectly observed God's holy commands. In fact, Jesus was obedient all the way to the cross, and therefore God exalted him to the highest place (Philippians 2:8-9). Though Adam had completely derailed the story, Christ got it back on track. Unfortunately, most people are still living in the corrupted story instead of the true one.

So how does someone enter Christ's story and escape Adam's twisted saga? The answer takes us back to the themes we explored in chapters 1 and 12 of this book. In the opener, we examined how the original gospel proclamation was "Jesus is Lord!" because of his mighty resurrection and ascension to the Father's right hand. We referred to this as the Christus Victor motif. We also looked in chapter 12 at how Irenaeus used the recapitulation idea to express the idea of a rightly ordered story. But what I haven't mentioned yet is Irenaeus's concept of the atonement. Let's take a look at his intriguing idea now.

Irenaeus believed that the incarnation offers human beings the opportunity to become one with Christ. Due to this spiritual unity, we possess what our Lord has: resurrection life and a mighty victory over sin, Satan, and death. "Our Lord Jesus Christ," said Irenaeus, "through His transcendent love [became] what we are, so that He might lead us to be what He Himself is."[1] This great exchange, when we finally reject our sly suitor Satan and enter into holy union with Jesus, fulfills the words of 1 Corinthians 15:22: "For as in Adam all die, so in Christ all will be made alive." Irenaeus's point was that for salvation to happen, you have to be *in* Christ. You have to believe in him, be baptized into him, follow him, obey him, partake of him, and mysteriously—or shall we say, *mystically*—be incorporated into him through the Holy Spirit. This is what the church fathers meant by mystical union with Christ: a total oneness that allows his saving benefits to pass to us.

Incarnation and Divinization

If Irenaeus of Lyon first emphasized the doctrine of union with Christ, two hundred years later, Athanasius of Alexandria perfected and completed it.[2] We saw in the last chapter that Athanasius understood sin as a corruptive and destructive force that was casting mankind into nonexistence. But God would not allow such a thing to happen to the creatures he had made in his image—an image shattered by sin. So God sent forth his Word to become flesh. Jesus of Nazareth, the God-Man, brought together the two parties that had become so terribly estranged: God and his creatures. Christ's true humanity allows him to be joined with us, while his true deity offers us an exalted destination to which we can ascend. When we are in union with Christ, we are in union with he who is fully God. The great riches he has, he shares with us (2 Corinthians 8:9). What a glorious thought! The intimate unity between Christ and his church caused the apostle Paul to observe, "This is a profound mystery" (Ephesians 5:32).

To express the saving truth of our exalted union with Christ, which seats us with our Lord in the heavenly places (Ephesians 2:6), Athanasius used a noteworthy expression. Referring to Jesus, he wrote, "He

---

1. *Against Heresies* 5. Preface.

2. Irenaeus started writing his *Against Heresies* in the AD 170s. Athanasius wrote continuously until his death in AD 373. Despite the two centuries between them, there was great continuity in their thought.

became a man so that we might become divine."[3] Now at first glance, this seems to be a very strange way of speaking. What did Athanasius mean when he said Christians can "become divine"? This sounds like one of those false religions that turns human beings into little gods. Did Athanasius intend such a thing? No way. He knew exactly what idolatry was, and he hated it. Far from uttering such blasphemy, Athanasius was emphasizing an important biblical theme. It is one that many evangelicals do not understand: The theology of divinization.

When sin is understood not just as legal guilt but as intrinsic disorder, and when Christ's saving work is not just a payment for sin but also a restorative union, it leads to a biblical theology of divinization. Again, this does not mean that humans can become little gods! We do not become members of the Holy Trinity; that is sacrilege. However, we do share in the life of the Trinity. In John 17:22-23, Jesus spoke to God the Father about his followers and said, "I have given them the glory that you gave me, that they may be one as we are one—I in them and you in me—so that they may be brought to complete unity."

Did you catch that? Jesus says that in him, we share in the Trinity's glory! We partake of the unity between the Father and the Son. Peter affirmed this same truth when he said that we can "participate in the divine nature" (2 Peter 1:4). The theology of divinization isn't a blasphemous trespass of the Creator/creature distinction. It is an incredible gift from a generous God, made possible only by our mystical union with Jesus. Being one with him means possessing what he has: The riches of divine life and a rightly ordered disposition. Salvation doesn't make us God—but it does make us godly.

Who can explain such wondrous truths? Although we can utter words about them, in the end, the reality of what is happening is beyond our comprehension. Yet just because it's mystical doesn't mean it's unreal. The fact is, Christians are joined to Jesus by the Holy Spirit. Through that indescribable union, we are elevated into the very throne room of God—indeed, into the glory of the Trinity itself. The apostle Paul was so amazed by this that he had to quote the prophet Isaiah: "No

---

3. *On the Incarnation* 54.3, translation mine.

eye has seen, no ear has heard, and no mind has imagined what God has prepared for those who love him" (1 Corinthians 2:9 NLT). So let's embrace the full mystery of our salvation. Instead of picking it apart with words, let's just enjoy our holy union with Jesus Christ.

> *In the past God hid this mystery, but now he has revealed it to his people. God wanted his people throughout the world to know the glorious riches of this mystery—which is Christ living in you, giving you the hope of glory.*
>
> COLOSSIANS 1:26-27 GOD'S WORD

20

You Aren't Truly Sorry
Until Your Body Is Sorry

hose are just empty words" we say when we suspect someone doesn't mean what they just told us. The expression reflects the fact that anyone can utter words easily or flippantly without being committed to the meaning behind the words. Speaking is easy, but backing it up takes effort.

I think back to the years when my two kids were young and they would get in a fight. It was up to me to bring them back together. Every parent has followed the same routine. It goes something like this:

> DAD: "Kids, you were both wrong. Say you're sorry to each other!"
>
> BROTHER, with arms crossed and lip curled, staring at the ground: "I'm sorry."
>
> SISTER, with an eye roll and a disgusted wag of head: "I'm sorry."

Does anyone think the two kids are actually sorry? Of course not. There's no repentance here. No desire for reconciliation and restoration. The kids in this scenario are just going through the motions because the parent is pressuring them. The important words "I'm sorry" are being uttered without any actual sorriness. In fact, continued hostility is still simmering beneath the surface.

We've all been there—and not just in the role of the cajoling parent trying to restore harmony between children. Even adults express contrition without actually making things right. Sometimes, of course, our words do reflect a change of heart. We actually do feel sorry for what we've done. But when the offense is serious—or when the one whom we've offended deserves far better treatment than what we've given them—does a feeling of regret in our hearts and a word of remorse on our lips go far enough? Or is some kind of action needed to bring full restoration?

In light of what I'm going to discuss in this chapter—the ancient Christian view that repentance requires actions and not just feelings—it's important to define at the outset what I am *not* saying. And here it is: I am not saying that saving faith requires added works of penance, or that any outward actions can earn us merit or favor with God. The gospel of grace requires nothing but faith alone. When we sin after salvation, then turn from it and ask God's forgiveness, he grants it to us freely and immediately. This is based on our appeal to the finished work of Christ, which is available to us at all times, for every sin, no matter how grave. "If we confess our sins, [God] is faithful and just and will forgive us our sins and purify us from all unrighteousness" (1 John 1:9).

But because we have received such lavish grace from God, it's all too easy to presume upon it. I believe evangelical Christianity is often guilty of this. In our desire to emphasize grace, we subtly cheapen it by not reminding ourselves of how serious our sin really is. We grab the grace without stopping to reflect on the price that was paid to obtain it. This doesn't make God grow tired of us, like the generous neighbor whose tools you borrow so often that he finally gets irked with your presumption. God's supply of mercy and grace is infinite. Instead, cheap grace devalues our own spiritual experience. When we don't let ourselves feel the magnitude of our wrongdoing—in our bodies as well as our souls—we lose a sense of the contrast between sin and grace. That's why it's healthy for us to take actions that put our sins before our eyes, not so we can wallow in them, but so we can rejoice all the more in the Savior who freed us from such degradation. Our deeds of repentance really do affect the disposition of our souls.

Embodied Actions

I think it's fair to say that ancient people put a greater emphasis on embodied actions than we do today. This wasn't just true for the ancient Christians, but for all people in those days. The things you did outwardly—especially in the religious realm—were connected to your inner self in a profound and mutually influential way. I am not sure why we have less awareness of this concept today. It might have to do with our modern, scientific worldview that doesn't believe in an immaterial soul. The typical secular view is that there is no soul within us, just brain chemistry that constructs a self-awareness which we call consciousness. As soon as the brain dies, this artificial byproduct of our synapses disappears.

Modern Christians, of course, do believe in a soul. But even then, we tend to think of the soul more like a future thing—the part of us that will go to heaven—than something relevant right now. Down here on earth, we pay greater attention to our physical bodies, often for the sake of attractive appearance, or at least for good health. Our eternal souls get less attention, receiving just a smattering of daily care through personal devotions or a few quick prayers winged up to the sky. In our day-to-day living, the body relates to one part of life, the soul to another. And since no one can see the flaws of our souls, we tend to pay greater attention to our bodies.

Increasingly, however, a purely mechanistic view of the human self is falling into disfavor. Scientists and physicians are finally rejecting the view that we are just biological machines. Today, modern people are starting to realize what the ancients already knew: That one's inner life is inseparable from the outer. Wellness gurus call this the mind-body connection. But what it really is, biblically speaking, is the soul-body connection. We were constructed by God with an intimate union between our body and soul (Genesis 2:7; 1 Thessalonians 5:23).

The church father Tertullian recommended a bodily action that would remind ancient believers of their faith all day long: making the sign of the cross on their foreheads.[1] By performing this physical gesture, a Christian would bring to mind the work of the Lord and embody a desire to live a cross-centered life. Tertullian suggested this action should be done when leaving or entering the house; when dressing or putting on shoes; when taking a bath; when eating a meal; when lighting lamps as the day comes to an end; and when going to bed at night. In other words, Tertullian reminds us to "pray without ceasing" (1 Thessalonians 5:17 ESV) and to mark our prayerfulness with physical actions that unite our words with our bodies. Imagine if every time you did a routine task, you also performed an outward gesture as a reminder of your higher calling. You'd be thinking about God so often that no action could ever become separated from his holy purposes!

The Penitential Process

The most important bodily actions for the ancient Christians weren't the daily habits like making the sign of the cross, but the more serious actions that signaled true repentance after falling into sin. What exactly is repentance? The Greek New Testament uses two main words. The first is *metanoia*, a change of mind. Repentance requires that we stop justifying ourselves and start thinking the way a holy God does about our sins. The second word is the verb *epistrephō*, which refers to a change of behavior (literally, "to make a turnaround"). "You turned to God from idols to serve the living and true God," Paul says in 1 Thessalonians 1:9. Repentance requires not just a different way of thinking, but a true conversion, a U-turn from your former deeds.

The Latin word for these concepts is *paenitentia*, from which we get the English words "repentance," "penance," and "penitential." The ancient church developed a formal process for helping its members go through the proper steps of repentance after they sinned (which today we call "church discipline"). When properly administered, this process wasn't about harsh judicial punishment but loving communal

---

1. *On the Military Crown* 3.

restoration. Just like pastors today, the ancient bishops recognized that holy chastisement is an important part of shepherding a flock. Of course, not every sin required the formal process of discipline and restoration. The daily sins that we all commit were to be handled by saying the Lord's Prayer: "Forgive us our debts, as we also have forgiven our debtors" (Matthew 6:12). But the larger and more impactful sins—violence, adultery, idolatry, and heresy—required the church's penitential process. What did that look like?

The person who had sinned grievously and wanted to make it right was enrolled in a special order of people called "penitents." These people confessed their sins publicly before the congregation, heeding the words of James 5:16, "Confess your sins to each other and pray for each other so that you may be healed" (see also Matthew 3:6; Acts 19:18).[2] This public confession wasn't just a restatement of the sins committed; it was also an act of humility in which the sinner asked for help from God and his people. Then, for a period of time whose length wasn't predetermined but was set by pastoral wisdom, the penitent would refrain from partaking of communion with the church. Instead, he or she would spend extra time in prayer, fasting, humble deeds of service, and giving generously to charity.

At last, when the time was right, the penitent would be received back into full communion. The bishop would lay hands on the restored person—what a glorious touch that would be!—and he or she would once again partake of the community's feast. Can you see how this process is not designed to punish a person but to bless them? Can you perceive the deep and lasting restoration that is being offered here? Can you feel the emotions of total release from sin, of full forgiveness, of powerful welcome and acceptance that such a process would produce? A Christian who has walked through a penitential journey like this gains greater freedom from lingering guilt than if someone used the word *grace* to make their forgiveness quick and easy. Penance isn't

---

2. Over time, the public confession in front of the church came to be viewed as too demanding, so confessing privately to pastor became the norm—eventually evolving into the confession booth that many people are familiar with in Roman Catholicism.

164 ◆ WISDOM from the ANCIENTS

designed to destroy, but to heal. And since we are whole creatures, the body has to experience this healing in addition to the soul.

Seasons of Penance

Because penance can be such a healing process, the ancient church developed regular fasts throughout the year when special focus could be given to penitential devotion. In chapter 28, we will look at the rise of a Christian calendar with liturgical seasons such as Lent. But here, let us simply observe that a penitential spirit doesn't have to be reserved for a formal church process after major sins. We can choose to enter into voluntary seasons of contrition, when heightened awareness of our sin and acts of bodily mortification can shape our souls in productive ways.

This type of spirituality is foreign to many evangelicals, but it isn't foreign to Scripture. Fasting, for example, has always been part of the spiritual life, both in ancient Israel and in church history. In 1 Samuel 7:6 we read, "On that day they fasted and there they confessed, 'We have sinned against the LORD.'" The Bible associates fasting with deep sorrow, which is precisely the emotion we ought to have when we consider the holiness of God and the bleakness of our sin. Yet the gospel turns our great sorrow into even greater joy. That is why the apostle Paul said, "Godly sorrow brings repentance that leads to salvation and leaves no regret" (2 Corinthians 7:10). Penance in the ancient church was designed to do exactly that: Leave no regret.

I will not deny that some dangers lurk here. There is a fine line between actions that embody our inner disposition of repentance and actions that we imagine will earn us approval with God. After all, in our human interactions we can sometimes obtain favor from powerful people by kissing up to them and doing whatever they want. It's easy to slip into the mindset that God is like that too. We erroneously start to think that along with the work of Christ, our righteous deeds help to satisfy God's demands for punishment or get us on his good side again. It is without doubt that certain penitential ideas of the ancient church led to the later belief that good works could earn saving merit with God. We must guard against this danger, for it is false doctrine.

Yet when all is said and done, the dangers are worth facing because the benefits are so real. As Christians, we know that forgiveness is freely available in Christ. But let's not turn free grace into cheap grace. When we choose to embody our sorrow for sin through penitential actions, we experience divine grace more fully. Do you see? The one who benefits here isn't God, but us. God has already forgiven us. He requires nothing more than the finished work of his Son. So penance is about helping us. The wise Christian will perform embodied actions when repenting of grievous sin. This isn't a legalistic burden upon us, but a beautiful opportunity for the whole self to experience the forgiveness that our Savior so freely offers.

> *Sorrow is better than laughter, for by sadness*
> *of face the heart is made glad.*
>
> ECCLESIASTES 7:3 ESV

21

Empires Are
Useful Temptations

Few people in the history of Christianity are more important than
Emperor Constantine. Most of the leading lights of church history
are famous because of their ideas about God, the Bible, and the church.
But Constantine's importance comes from his power to create change.
He was the first Roman emperor to accept Jesus as his deity instead of
the pagan gods. He put an end to persecution. And he started the process that made Christianity the official religion of Rome.

As we consider the life and impact of Constantine in this chapter—
and thus the church's relationship with the state[1]—it is helpful to
begin by understanding how this influential emperor has been viewed
by later generations. On the one hand, he has been celebrated as the
founder of Christendom, a political arrangement in which the church
is intertwined with politicians and government officials. On the other
hand, Constantine introduced a dramatic shift that many have interpreted as "the fall of the church." Today, some people praise the church-
state cooperation that Constantine brought, while others decry it as
compromise and apostasy.

---

1. I use the word *state* to describe government in general, not in the more technical sense of nation
   states, which did not exist until the late modern period.

But instead of viewing these issues from a modern perspective, let's view it through the eyes—or should I say, *eye*—of a particular ancient Christian. The godly bishop Paphnutius was pastoring his church along the Nile River when he was arrested by one of Constantine's political enemies, Maximinus Daia. This depraved brute was in the habit of maiming Christian leaders by disabling an arm or a leg, then condemning them to a long, slow death by hard labor in the imperial mines. Bishop Paphnutius's left hamstring was sliced at the knee and his right eye was gouged out. For a long time, he slaved away in the mines, limping around in the darkness, half starved, performing back-breaking work every day.

But then Constantine came to power. As a pro-Christian emperor, one of his first policies was to end persecution and free those who were suffering for their faith. Several ancient sources attest that he gave special honor to Paphnutius after releasing him from the mines. One writer tells us, "The emperor honored this man exceedingly, and often sent for him to the palace, and kissed the part where the eye had been torn out. So great a devoutness characterized the emperor Constantine."[2] The fact that a Roman emperor in all his majesty would kiss the empty eye socket of a crippled old man says something about who Constantine was. For the Christians who lived in such dark times, this wasn't the fall of the church but a triumphant victory over its persecutors.

To put this in terms we can understand today, let's imagine some historical events that didn't actually happen but would have been wonderful if they did. In our fictional scenario, a godly Christian leader rises up in Nazi Germany against Hitler. This leader is able to defeat the Nazis halfway through their reign of terror. The new Christian leader frees the Jews from concentration camps and saves millions of lives from the Holocaust. He also releases Dietrich Bonhoeffer from prison, not only preventing his martyrdom but actually making him the chief adviser for German religious affairs. With Bonhoeffer at his side, this imaginary Christian leader plans to rule Germany with strong support for the church and religious freedom for all. Wouldn't this be a good thing?

2. Socrates Scholasticus, *Ecclesiastical History* 1.11.

Of course it would. But it would also be—let us not deny it—a sore temptation to the church. Part of what gave the Christians of Nazi Germany their identity was their need to stand as the Confessing Church against an evil regime. But what if we took that enemy away and gave the church power, prestige, and money instead? Would those Christians have been able to resist the temptation? Perhaps they could have. Their inner moral compass might have remained strong. Then they could have used their influence and resources to bless their society.

Or perhaps they would have gone soft. The power and money might have corrupted them. That is an ever-present danger for Christians who run in high circles. Even so, would anyone choose to remain under persecution just to avoid those temptations? If you were Dietrich Bonhoeffer, would you have chosen to be hung by the neck in Hitler's brutal gulag? Or would you have chosen to be freed so you could help lead the new Germany? What about the ancient church? If you were Paphnutius, would you have chosen to stagger around in a dark mine until you died of exhaustion? Or would you have gladly returned to your former home and tried to help Constantine govern well?

I'm sure you can see the dilemma here. The power of empire is useful for spreading the gospel and advancing the common good. Yet it is also a deadly temptation to a righteous soul.

"In This Sign, You Shall Conquer."

Emperor Constantine came to power through some of the most famous events in church history. In the early 300s, the Roman Empire was ruled by four emperors in separate quadrants—and no one agreed on who those four should be. This led to a lot of civil war. Constantine found himself opposed by his brother-in-law, Maxentius. Since war loomed between them, Constantine decided to take the initiative and march down from the Rhineland to battle in Rome.

But a few years earlier—not on the march to Rome as many people erroneously suppose—something dramatic had happened in the sky that Constantine interpreted as a miracle. Historians think the event might have been a solar halo that formed rings around the sun and made crisscrossed rays in it. Whatever it was, Constantine took it as a sign of victory from the sun god. At first, he thought this god was Apollo. But then a second event took place that caused him to change his mind about the sender of the omen.

The church historian Eusebius, who knew Constantine personally, tells us what happened. He says that while the emperor was pondering what the sign could mean, night fell, and,

> in his sleep the Christ of God appeared to him with the same sign which he had seen in the heavens [i.e., a cross], and commanded him to make a likeness of that sign which he had seen in the heavens, and to use it as a safeguard in all engagements with his enemies. At dawn, [Constantine] arose and communicated the marvel to his friends. And then, calling together the workers in gold and precious stones, he sat in the midst of them, and described to them the figure of the sign he had seen, bidding them to represent it in gold and precious stones...The emperor constantly made use of this sign of salvation as a safeguard against every adverse and hostile power, and commanded that others similar to it should be carried at the head of all his armies.[3]

This famous battle standard came to be known as the labarum. Its primary symbol was the Christogram: the crisscrossed Greek letter *chi* (X) overlaid by the letter *rho* (P), forming the symbol ☧. These are the first two letters in the word *Christ*.

With this banner leading his army, and with his soldiers' shields also marked with the sign of the cross, Constantine was ready for battle. In the spring of AD 312, the troops crossed the Alps, and in late October they engaged Maxentius at the Milvian Bridge over the Tiber River a few miles outside of Rome. Although Constantine's army was smaller, he nonetheless managed to push the enemy forces back into the river. Maxentius was drowned, and Constantine fished the corpse out of the water. After sticking his brother-in-law's head on the end of a spear, he rode into the city as a conqueror and liberator.

---

3. *Life of Constantine* 1.29–31.

Later, he would tell Eusebius that the cross he saw in the noonday sun was such a vivid sign that its message to him was clear: "Conquer by this." Subsequent writers and artists assumed that the words themselves were written across the sky, though Constantine probably never said this.

Imperial Christianity

For the next 25 years of his life, Constantine pursued a policy of active support for the church. One of his first deeds after his great victory was to issue a letter of toleration to his governors, a document now called the Edict of Milan. This text commanded that Christians—in fact, all people—should have absolute freedom to worship the Supreme God however they wished. Symbolically, the edict marks the end of ancient church persecution. From that point on, there would be no more, "Christians to the lions!"

But Constantine went beyond simple toleration. Another of his immediate actions was to open the imperial treasury to the church. He exempted bishops from taxes and burdensome civic obligations, and he started a flow of money for a church building program across the empire (see chapter 26). He also convened the important Council of Nicaea to define the doctrine of the Trinity (see chapter 23). Constantine passed laws that fit with Christian values, such as making Sunday a day of rest; instituting protections for orphans and vulnerable children; and protecting the rights of slaves.[4] He weakened the pagan religious system as much as he could and didn't sponsor the widespread building of temples. Instead, he focused—through the influence of his mother, Helena—on the Holy Land, where he built monumental new churches (see chapter 29).

Yet at what cost did these good things come? For the first time in Christian history, wars were being waged in the name of Jesus. This would prompt the ancient church to consider what might constitute a

---

4. Constantine did not, however, abolish slavery. To this day, no one has been able to completely rid the earth of this evil practice.

"just war." While I believe such a thing does exist—a properly constituted state action that directs force against evil aggressors—I also have to admit that a lot of history's supposedly Christian wars were anything but just. It was the holy-war mentality that led, seven centuries after Constantine, to the atrocities of the Crusades. As is so often the case when Christians have power, in an attempt to do good, great evil can be committed.

Another negative aspect of Constantine's rise to power was the watering down of the church's fervor compared to earlier centuries. When Christian conversion came with the cost of possible persecution, only the most committed people would dare to join the faith. But now it was expedient for everyone to join the emperor's favored religion. This led to a lot of nominal Christians who converted in theory but didn't actually experience a change of heart. At the upper end of society, it produced superficial Christians who gave lip service to the faith but still lived in self-indulgence and indifference to the poor. The great preacher John Chrysostom railed against people like these, calling them out for their luxurious living and lack of true Christian morality. Eventually, John's prophetic preaching against the elites got him sent into exile, leading to his death. The problem of cultural Christianity has never truly disappeared within the church.

The Enigma of Empire

Today in the city of Rome, atop the Capitoline Hill where Jupiter's temple once crowned the highest point, stands a museum that contains a colossal marble bust of Constantine. The giant head was formerly part of a statue that depicted the seated emperor holding a device in his hand. By some accounts, the object was a pole with a horizontal bar—a typical Roman battle standard. By other accounts, it was a Christian cross. Which was it?

It was both, of course. The cross can easily become a civic emblem— and therein lies the enigma of Christianity's relationship to empire. On the one hand, the power of the state to do good is undeniable. Laws aren't just vague ideas that sit in dusty books in the capital city. Laws have consequences, and if Christians can influence them in the right direction, real benefits will accrue and people will flourish. In lands that respect religious liberty, the gospel can go forward without hindrance. When economic prosperity occurs, families are stable, funds are available for charity, and beautiful works of art can be made.

Yet empire always comes with a cost. Its gods—whether represented by idols or dollars—will demand their due. The church must never forget this insidious idolatry, and so never forget to retain its militant and prophetic stance against the powers in high places. How do Christians remain "in the world" (John 15:19)—fully engaged in a public life that includes economics and politics—yet not be "of the world" in ways that compromise our values or tempt us to bow down to false deities?

There is no easy answer to this question. Each dilemma must be faced in turn, to be sorted out by each Christian generation with wisdom and caution. Yet at the very least, we can remember the central lesson of the ancient church's encounter with Constantine. Empire has the power to bless or to destroy—and the two are never far apart.

Jesus said to them, "Render to Caesar the things that are Caesar's,
and to God the things that are God's." And they marveled at him.
MARK 12:17 ESV

22

God Refuses to Be
a Helicopter Parent

Like many parents, I vividly remember the first day I let my son drive our car. Handing him the keys to the family sedan was an exercise in pure faith. Even in an empty parking lot, I thought this mad speedster would surely crash into something. It didn't matter that there were no other cars around. Hitting a curb at 30 miles per hour could do plenty of damage too. Although nothing terrible ended up happening that day, still, the feeling of putting your car—or even your life—into a fifteen-year-old's hands is unnerving.

Our heavenly Father, of course, isn't scared like this. He is sovereign and all-knowing, so he isn't alarmed by our miscues or surprised by our whims. Yet his sovereignty doesn't mean he prevents us from making a mess along the way. Failures and faults, losses and lapses, bungles and botches…these are all part of our growth process. And the thing about God is, he's good with that. God is a risk-taking God. He's willing to put big tasks in the hands of the church and let us fail our way to success. Messy processes don't bother him. Wandering journeys don't deter him. He just keeps guiding his people by the light of the Spirit. And eventually, he works all things together for good.

Eventually.

In this chapter, I'd like to suggest that one of the biggest tasks God ever put into the hands of the church was determining which books are supposed to be in his Holy Bible. He didn't have to do it that way. He could have floated the books down from heaven. Or written them in scintillating ink that no one could deny was divine. At the very least, he could have told some great prophet like Moses, Isaiah, or John, "Take up your pen and write down the following books that belong in my Word." But God didn't do that. Like a risk-taking parent who refuses to hover and micromanage, he let the church figure it out. The whole process took about four hundred years. Yet with God's Spirit indwelling his attentive people, it worked.

What Is a Canon?

The term we use for the 66 books that make up the Bible is *canon*. Like so many other terms from the ancient church, it's a Greek word: *kanōn*. Normally, it's translated into English as "rule," as in Galatians 6:16, "for all who walk by this rule, peace and mercy be upon them" (ESV). The literal meaning of *kanōn* was a straight reed or bar that carpenters used for measuring lengths, like a yardstick. The symbolism of a measuring rod is obvious. Things that belong to a "canon" are things that measure up to God's standard.

In the second century, the ancient believers began to speak of the "canon/rule of faith." We saw in chapter 14 that this term described the brief summary of theology that eventually became known as the Apostles' Creed. So the word *kanōn* described the doctrines that met the divine standard. Unlike the nonsense of the heretics, the content in the church's creed or rule of faith was an accurate synopsis of Christian truth.

One common tactic of the heretics was to use strange books about Jesus that the mainline church did not accept. Today, historians refer to these texts as the Gnostic gospels, along with other associated writings. By the end of the second century, these writings had spread everywhere. There was a serious need to define which books the church should use in its public worship and which should be rejected because they were full of Gnosticism or other false doctrine.

The term *canon* came to describe the acceptable books because they contained the same ideas as the church's creed. This was the core message that the church had always proclaimed, ever since the apostles began preaching the gospel. So the "rule of faith" was, first, the apostolic message of Jesus Christ, and second, the writings that contained this message. *Kanōn* meant both of these things, with the creedal meaning eventually including the textual meaning as well.

Now the stage was set for a debate over which books did or did not contain the apostolic message. The Lord used godly believers to help clarify the truth. It took a long time—almost four centuries, as I mentioned above—to determine it. It also took a lot of study. But most of all, it took the Holy Spirit working silently and gradually in the church to make the matter clear. Let's take a closer look at the messy process that God allowed to unfold. He was willing to sit back and let his Spirit-filled children figure out which books belonged in the canon of Scripture.

The Old Testament Canon

In the process of determining the canon of the Old Testament, the early Christians had an obvious group to interact with: the Jews, who cared just as much as the Christians did about which books were in or out. The Jewish teachers had been having this debate since long before Christianity began. Historians today are uncertain about when exactly the canon[1] of the Hebrew Scriptures was "closed," that is, when the Jewish authorities agreed on what it contained. The answer to this question is elusive because different communities had different views at different times.

However, the one thing we can say with certainty is that the Jewish canon had a threefold structure during the time of Jesus. We know this because he referred to it as, "the Law of Moses, the Prophets and the Psalms" (Luke 24:44). Soon after this, the most common terms for

---

1. The rabbis didn't use the term *canon*. Instead, they debated which books "defiled the hands." This meant the books were so holy that you couldn't handle them carelessly. It was the rabbinic way to describe which books had inspired status and which were merely human works.

178 ◆ WISDOM from the ANCIENTS

the threefold division became "the Law, the Prophets, and the Writings." During the ancient church era, the Jews agreed about what was in the Law (the five books of Moses) and the Prophets (Joshua, Judges, Samuel, Kings, Isaiah, Jeremiah, Ezekiel, and the 12 minor prophets). Everything else was lumped into the Writings. Most of those books were undisputed and authoritative, especially the Psalms. Yet there was ongoing rabbinic debate about Esther, the Song of Songs, and Ecclesiastes.

By the end of the ancient church era (around AD 500), the dust had finally settled and agreement had been reached. The Jewish writing known as the Talmud listed the same books we include in our Old Testament today. From then on, these books and no others comprised the Hebrew Scriptures of the Jews. Likewise, the ancient Christians accepted the 39 books of today's Old Testament as canonical. Although the Jews and Christians had different orders and names for these books, they agreed on the central point: The Hebrew writings from Genesis to Malachi are God's Word.

But the prophet Malachi didn't end his ministry at the very moment that the Virgin Mary conceived the Christ child in her womb. In other words, the New Testament doesn't pick up where the Old leaves off. There is a gap of about 450 years between the two. During this period, the Jews began to write in Greek. Some of these new texts were included in the Greek version of the Old Testament that the Christians liked to use, known as the Septuagint. Because of this, there was some debate in the ancient church about whether these Greek books also belonged in the canon.

One ancient Christian who investigated this issue was Melito, bishop of Sardis. Melito decided to visit the Holy Land around AD 170 to find out the facts for himself. After making the trip and investigating Jewish and Christian beliefs on the matter, he reported that the Old Testament consists of the very same books we have today (except he omitted Esther). Melito did not include the extra books of the Greek Septuagint in his list.[2]

---

2. It is possible that Melito may have accepted the book *Wisdom of Solomon* along with Proverbs, depending on how we interpret his words. See Eusebius, *Church History* 4.26.13–14.

In the fourth century, the great linguistic scholar Jerome made a Latin translation of the Bible that was widely used in subsequent centuries. Known as the Vulgate, this Bible included the extra books of the Old Testament, but Jerome clearly stated that they should hold lesser authority. However, later generations of Latin-speaking Christians tended to ignore this guidance and treat the extra books as equal to the other 39. In this decision, they were supported by many church fathers who believed the Greek books should be counted as scriptural along with the Hebrew ones. For example, Augustine of Hippo included these books in his canon list.[3]

It was only with the Reformation in the 1500s that Christians began to question once again the wide acceptance of these extra books. Protestant leaders such as Martin Luther and John Calvin reverted to the ancient view of Jerome and the Jews that only the Hebrew books should be counted as God's Word. They called the extra books "apocrypha," which means writings that are "hidden away" and not to be used in public church worship. Although they could be printed in Bibles, they were not in the canon. The Roman Catholic Church responded to the Protestants in 1546 by officially including these books as a secondary part of the Old Testament canon.

Although I wish to show respect to my Catholic friends whose view has considerable support from church history, I believe the Protestant view is the correct definition of the canon.[4] And I marvel when I think about what this means. God was willing to let this important debate unfold over a very long time—not just in the ancient church era, but all the way up to the 1500s and beyond! Clearly, God doesn't want to solve these mysteries for us by miraculous intervention. He is no helicopter parent who maneuvers us toward the desired outcome. Instead, he lets us rely on his Holy Spirit and wrestle with big issues over time—even

---

3. *On Christian Teaching* 2.8.13.

4. Why do I accept the Protestant canon? Partly because the Jewish rabbis didn't see fit to accept the Greek books into their canon either; and partly because those books contain some historical errors. The evidence from figures like Melito of Sardis that the earliest Christians didn't accept these books is also persuasive to me. But the main reason for my view is that Jesus himself accepts the threefold division of the Old Testament (Luke 24:44) and he does not give authority to the "apocrypha."

if it means a whole lot of people will get it wrong. God trusts his children to work out these issues in church history.

What About the New Testament?

The early Christians soon became aware that their new covenant received from Jesus was described in specific writings that formed a New Testament (the Greek word for "covenant" and "testament" are the same; see 2 Corinthians 3:6). Now the question was: Which books should be included in God's second Testament? The fake Gnostic writings had to be distinguished from the original, apostolic ones.

Sometime around the end of the second century, an unknown person attempted to define the New Testament canon by writing out a list of the proper books. This anonymous list survives in a Latin fragment discovered by an Italian scholar in 1740. Called the Muratorian Canon in honor of its discoverer, Lodovico Muratori, the list shows that the canon was still under development in ancient times. It properly includes the four Gospels, Acts, the Pauline epistles, and two of John's epistles. Yet it omits Hebrews, James, the letters of Peter, and 3 John. It also includes two extra books that shouldn't be there. So the Muratorian Canon was a step in the right direction, but not the final word.

Our friend Athanasius (whom we met in chapter 18) was the first man we know to have recorded the proper New Testament canon. In the year 367, he wrote a pastoral letter to his Egyptian flock to tell them which books are part of God's Word. After giving the correct list, he declared, "These are fountains of salvation, that they who thirst may be satisfied with the living words they contain. In these alone is proclaimed the doctrine of godliness. Let no man add to these, neither let him take away from these."[5] Thirty years later, a major council at the African city of Carthage ratified this same list. So we can say that by the year 397, the Christian church had finally agreed on its New Testament canon—four hundred years after its Savior was born!

---

5. *Easter Letter* 39.5–6. As for the Old Testament, Athanasius omits Esther and adds two extra works. Though he denies that the rest of the Greek works from the Septuagint are part of the canon, he says they are acceptable for Christian edification.

All this reveals something important about how God works. His primary method isn't to use individual superheroes but the whole Christian community. The Spirit dwells in the church, and God points us toward truth through the collective wisdom of his people. He is willing to trust us with big things, not only with regard to the canon but other conundrums as well. What great issues face the church today? Do you think we'll make a mess of it? Count on it! But also know that God is with us in the mess. Whether our issues are resolved today or not for another thousand years, we can be certain that Jesus' promise is true: "I am with you always, to the end of the age" (Matthew 28:20 NASB).

> *I have much more to say to you, more than you*
> *can now bear. But when he, the Spirit of truth,*
> *comes, he will guide you into all the truth.*
>
> JOHN 16:12-13

23

Without the Trinity, Everyone Stops Short of Heaven

I n northern New Hampshire stands a mountain at 6,288 feet of elevation known as Mount Washington. While this is not an extremely tall mountain compared to other peaks around the globe, its northern latitude, proximity to the Atlantic Ocean, and prominence above the local terrain all combine to give it some of the most dramatic weather on the planet. In addition to torrential rain and deep snow, Mount Washington is known for its especially fierce winds. The observatory atop the summit registered a wind chill temperature of -97°F in 2018. In 1934, a gust blew at 231 miles per hour—the second highest wind speed ever recorded on earth outside of a tornado.

Yet despite Mount Washington's ferocious weather, the mountain has been tamed by humans—or so I once believed. An auto road takes travelers 7.6 miles to the summit, earning them the right to use a bumper sticker that celebrates the achievement. I remember riding up that road one summer day many years ago. My brother was driving beside his wife, and my wife and I were in the back seat. As we neared the peak, the sky grew ominous. Though it made my wife nervous, I wanted to press on. Clearly, even motorists can get a case of "summit fever"— the compulsive urge to make it to the top of mountain. But then rain began to fall, so my brother turned the car around and we headed back down. To this day, the summit of Mount Washington taunts me for having fallen short.

Of course, failing to reach a mountain peak during a leisurely drive isn't the end of the world. But when it comes to salvation—well, that's an area where you definitely want to make it all the way. The ancient church fathers understood this, which is why they took their theological disputes so seriously. Theology wasn't just trivia to be debated in a classroom. The words you believed and preached to the lost—these things truly mattered. Even a single letter could make the difference between life and death.

In this chapter, we'll wrestle along with the ancient church as they tried to understand the Trinity. The Christian description of the Father, Son, and Holy Spirit couldn't just be a new kind of polytheism. Many Roman towns had a threefold temple to Jupiter, Juno, and Minerva on the main square, and the Christians didn't want any part of that. They didn't believe in three separate gods cooperating in a heavenly council. Like the Jews before them, the Christians embraced the principle of Deuteronomy 6:4, "Hear, O Israel: The Lord our God, the Lord is one."

But as strict monotheists, the Christians had a problem that the Jews never faced: They also believed "Jesus is Lord" because of his resurrection. This meant Jesus was more than just a man. Somehow, he was a divine man, in a way that wasn't exactly clear. He was the Son of God. He was the Christ, the Messiah, the Anointed One. He was the Word who was there in the beginning (John 1:1). So if the Father and Son could both be called God—as well as the Holy Spirit to make a "trinity"—how could you believe that and still be a monotheist? In the ancient church period, many explanations were offered. But only one of them was correct, and today's Nicene Creed expresses it. This chapter is about how that story unfolded—and why it matters.

False Starts and Dead Ends

The first generation of church fathers didn't do a lot of speculating about the issues I've just raised. They only repeated biblical statements and were content with that. While this approach might seem wise, in the end, it doesn't work. We can't just repeat words without comprehending them. The church needs to understand exactly what the Bible teaches about its God. So, starting in the second century, Christian thinkers began to wrestle with the important issue of how God can be both one and three.

One solution to this conundrum came from some Jewish Christians. They claimed that Jesus was a normal man whom God "adopted." The adoptionists found a basis for their view in the account of Jesus' baptism. According to Luke 3:22, the voice of God said, "You are my beloved Son; with you I am well pleased" (ESV). However, some Bible manuscripts of this verse instead quoted Psalm 2:7: "You are my son; today I have become your father." So the adoptionist idea was that God chose Jesus at his baptism for a special divine role. But this isn't what the Bible teaches. Jesus wasn't a regular man whom God elevated into the status of sonship. Just the opposite: The eternal Son of God came down to earth and became a human being. He started high and went low; he didn't get elevated from normal humanity into the divine realm. Adoptionism isn't correct.

A second false start toward understanding the Trinity came from a group that scholars today call "modalists." In ancient times, they were called "monarchians," which means they saw God as a monarch, or a single ruler. To a certain extent, that's true, right? All Christians must believe that God is one (James 2:19).

Unfortunately, modalism doesn't adequately distinguish the three persons of the Trinity from one another. The modalists said that sometimes God is experienced as a Father, sometimes as a Son, sometimes as a Spirit—as if each is just a different aspect of the same personality. Think of a three-sided pyramid, such as the child's toy which is similar to a Rubik's Cube but triangular in shape. If you placed this toy (known as a Pyraminx) in your palm and turned it, you would see three sides of the same structure. But God isn't like this. Jesus isn't a "side" of the Father—he is someone else. Both are distinct individuals. Their relationship is marked by other-love, not self-love. The same is true of the Holy Spirit. So modalism can't be correct because it doesn't allow for interpersonal love. Each member of the Trinity is a distinct person, not a personality trait of the same being. The oneness of God cannot be allowed to destroy his threeness.

A third and final false start came from the man who began the whole controversy that led to the Council of Nicaea. This man was the Egyptian heretic Arius. By all accounts, he was an intelligent, persuasive, and earnest pastor in Alexandria. But being likeable doesn't excuse you from heresy. Every heretic is earnest in his or her beliefs. And Arius was earnestly committed to a view that was dead wrong.

In the year 318 or thereabouts, Arius publicly confronted his bishop, Alexander, over a point of doctrine. When Alexander stated—correctly—that Jesus is an eternal being, Arius rebuked him and said Jesus wasn't eternal.[1] So what was he, then? If something isn't eternal, it must have been created by something that came before it. And that is what Arius believed about Jesus: He was a creation of the Father.

Arius's slogan was, "There was when he was not." In other words, there was a time when Jesus didn't exist. While Arius accepted that Jesus was the first and most glorious thing that God ever made, still, he wasn't eternal. Therefore he wasn't fully God. Jesus was a lesser kind of deity, a secondary god that the true God had made to accomplish his purposes. For teaching this scandalous view, Arius was kicked out of his home church in Alexandria. But he found welcome elsewhere, and soon the whole church was debating the Arian view.[2]

The Council of Nicaea

Due to this theological controversy, the one, holy, catholic, and apostolic church had been split into two factions, for and against Arianism (with numerous subfactions that had slightly different takes on the matter). The main dividing line was whether or not Jesus was

---

1. I am using the term *Jesus* in this chapter to describe the second person of the Trinity. Often in these debates, the ancient fathers referred to him as the "Word," or *logos*, based on the term John used in his Gospel.

2. The "Arian" view has nothing to do with the white supremacist or neo-Nazi use of the term "Aryan."

co-eternal with the Father, and therefore equal in his divinity. Was Jesus "true God" or a secondary god?

Emperor Constantine had just gained control of the whole Roman Empire at the time this debate broke out. He desperately wanted the Christian faith, not old paganism, to be the spiritual glue that held his realm together. Imagine his frustration when he discovered that the faith that had been so marked by catholic unity was now split by theology! At times, the debate hinged on a single Greek letter, the *iota*, which could change the word "same" into "similar." The ancient church was divided over whether Jesus shared the same divinity as God the Father or only had a similar kind of divinity. Such great dissension had to be resolved—and Constantine was willing to pay for it. He ordered all the bishops to travel at imperial expense to his lakeside palace at Nicaea. They were to arrive by the summer of 325 so they could come up with a permanent solution.

Around 300 bishops and other leaders showed up for the great event. Many of them, like Paphnutius whom we met in an earlier chapter, were maimed or crippled from having survived the persecution that Constantine had only recently put to an end. One bishop couldn't use his hands because red-hot irons had damaged the nerves. Others had lost eyes or limbs. "In short, the council looked like an assembled army of martyrs," remarked one ancient historian.[3] This reminds us of the seriousness that marked such an important occasion.

The debates at Nicaea lasted all summer, and we don't really know the details. What we do know is the final outcome. The Nicene council produced a creed that confirmed the view of Bishop Alexander and his devoted protégé Athanasius. This creed states in no uncertain terms that Jesus is fully God:

> We believe in one Lord Jesus Christ, the Son of God, the only-begotten of the Father, that is, of the substance of the Father; God from God, Light from Light, true God

---

3. Theodoret of Cyrus, *Ecclesiastical History* 1.6.

from true God, begotten, not made, consubstantial with
the Father.[4]

Notice that the creed says Jesus is "true God from true God," and "not
made." These phrases rejected the heresies of Arius. Yet the creed's most
important expression was "consubstantial with the Father." In Greek,
the key word is *homoousios*, "of the same substance." If two things share
the same substance, one can't exist before the other. The Father God
and the Son of God are co-eternal.

Later, a final form of the Nicene Creed expressed more clearly the
full deity of the Holy Spirit as well. In this way, the biblical doctrine of
the Trinity came to its proper expression, and it has been held by faithful Christians ever since. Now the Arian view was defeated. Though
it lingered for a while like a smoldering forest fire before finally being
extinguished, the Nicene council had clearly rejected it. The creed concludes, "Those who say, 'There was a time when he was not'…the catholic and apostolic church of God condemns."

Going All the Way

Why does this stuff matter? Isn't it just meaningless quibbling about
words? Not at all. The gospel hinges on these words! According to the
Arian view of salvation, our fellow creature Jesus models for us what
we can aspire to be. He shows us how to be obedient so we can climb
up to heaven after him. Arius believed in salvation through imitating
the life of Jesus, who wasn't God in the flesh, but just a creature striving
to be good like the rest of us. Salvation in Arianism consists of moral
growth toward perfection. And that is not the gospel.

For Athanasius, on the other hand, salvation requires that the Son
of God be fully and completely God. Through our union with Christ,
we humans, by grace, are invited to share in the life of the Holy Trinity.
But this requires that he to whom we are united, our Lord and Savior
Jesus Christ, must be consubstantial with the Father in order to make

---

4. Socrates Scholasticus, *Ecclesiastical History* 1.8.

our heavenly union complete. If Jesus falls short, so do we. If he is less than fully God, he can only take us partway. Like my experience at Mount Washington, we would be turned back shy of the summit. That isn't salvation. It is a failure that causes us to tumble into hell.

But let us rejoice! In Christ, we do not fail. Our Lord Jesus is fully God. The three persons of the Trinity are co-eternal and consubstantial. When the Spirit unites us to Jesus at salvation, we aren't joined to a demigod who falls short, but to a Savior who takes us all the way home.

May the grace of the Lord Jesus Christ, and the love of God,
and the fellowship of the Holy Spirit be with you all.

2 Corinthians 13:14

A Bridge Only Works
When It Has Two Ends

Recently I had the opportunity to drive along the stunning section of the California coastline known as Big Sur. The winding highway hugs the cliffs that loom above the Pacific Ocean, giving expansive views of the sea and incredible vistas of the rugged and rocky shore. One of the highlights of the drive is the Bixby Creek Bridge, a long, arched span that crosses a deep ravine. Tourists (myself included) often stop along the roadside to take pictures of the scenic bridge. It has graced that marvelous spot on the Big Sur Highway since 1932.

Of course, the bridge only works because both ends are connected to the highway on either side. Imagine a bridge that didn't lead smoothly onto the road—it would be a disaster! We actually have bridges like that here in the city of Chicago where I work. Starting in the 1830s, mechanical drawbridges were built to span the Chicago River at various street crossings. Today many of them are still dotted around the city. Sometimes they open in the middle like a typical drawbridge that allows tall boats to pass under the center. Others (used mostly for train tracks) pivot up from one end, like the bridges over a moat at a medieval castle. If someone drove onto the raised leaf of a drawbridge at full speed, their car would fly off the end of the ramp, curve in a graceful arc for a second or two, then crash and burn on the opposite pavement,

192 ◆ WISDOM from the ANCIENTS

or maybe sink into the murky depths forever. Bridges don't work when they aren't connected at both ends!

The Bible refers to Jesus as a bridge maker. No, I'm not talking about a carpentry job he might have had in Nazareth. I mean the bridge between God and humanity. In 1 Timothy 2:5, we read, "There is one God and one mediator between God and mankind, the man Christ Jesus." The Greek word for "mediator" is *mesitēs*, a person who acts as a go-between or a broker between two parties. It is related to the word for being "in the middle." The epistle to the Hebrews links Jesus' role as the mediator of a new covenant with his position as our great High Priest (Hebrews 8:6; 9:15; 12:24). Priests are people who go between the divine and human realms. We see this especially in the Latin word for priest: *pontifex*, literally, a "bridge maker." The Bible calls Jesus the bridge between sinful humans and a loving God.

The ancient Christians understood that Jesus was their only pathway to eternal life. That's why they labored so much over the correct way to describe him. They knew their salvation depended on getting their Christology just right. Some Christians wanted to emphasize Jesus' humanity—the fact that he's down here with us in the grit and grime of life. Others wanted to emphasize his deity—the great truth that he came from glory on high. So which one is right? Both are essential! Just like the Bixby Creek Bridge, both ends have to connect to solid ground. A bridge can't be an either-or sort of thing. It has to be both-and. So too, Jesus has to be both God and Man. Because if he's not, our bridge maker can't take us from one place and lead us to where we need to go.

Fully Divine—Now What?

Let's think back to the previous chapter on the doctrine of the Trinity. In that chapter, I used a different car-driving analogy. I wrote about not reaching the peak of Mount Washington, an example of falling short. The theological question that the ancient church debated with regard to the Trinity was whether Jesus fell short of full deity. Was he completely God or only partially so? Arius said, "No, he isn't equal to God, just a glorious creature." But Athanasius said, "Yes, he's fully divine just like God the Father." And that is the correct, biblical view. Jesus is co-eternal and consubstantial with the Father.

Over the course of the fourth century, the church fathers hashed out the details of what this meant. The result was the Nicene Creed, whose final version from the year 381 declared that the Father, Son, and Holy Spirit are equally divine. The fourth century ended with Emperor Theodosius issuing a decree, the Edict of Thessalonica, that made Trinitarian Christianity the official religion of the Roman Empire. Ever since that moment, throughout all of church history, only heretics and false religions have tried to claim that Jesus is some kind of inferior demigod. True Christians do not believe that. They believe Jesus is 100 percent divine.

When the fifth century began (the AD 400s), the theological questions about Jesus turned to the next important topic: What about his *humanity?* Since Jesus is now understood to be fully and completely God, should we also say he's a real man? Or did he just seem to be human? Was he some kind of glorified man, different than us mortals? Was his physical body just a shell that he put on like a hermit crab, but it wasn't truly part of him? Or was he a complete man with a body and soul like ours, except without sin? Are there two separate personalities in Jesus—the divine Son of God who cooperates with the carpenter from Nazareth to accomplish salvation? Or should we think of Jesus as a single, unified being?

Do you sense the complexity here? Christology presented some thorny issues that took a lot of effort to work out. In fact, as we'll see, the church fathers were divided into two main camps. But as is so often the case when it comes to doctrine, holding two truths in tension is essential. Jesus has to be fully God. He also has to be fully man. Theologically, we can't deny either one. That's why the analogy of driving over a bridge works for this chapter. "The left end is most important!" someone might say. "No, I prefer the right end!" replies someone else. "Left!" and "Right!" they shout back and forth. But what does the driver say—the person who has to cross the deep ravine? "Both ends matter to me!" And that's the truth. A bridge only gets you to safety when it has two solid ends. Neither side is more important than the other.

Antioch: City of the Human Jesus

Early on, a Christological view developed in the city of Antioch that emphasized the true manhood of Jesus—an essential theological truth. But over time, this view began to run into some problems. Because the Antiochians knew that Jesus was also God, they tried to add his divine part while keeping his manhood separate. This had the unfortunate effect of setting up two aspects of Jesus that functioned as distinct personalities. Let me illustrate why that just doesn't work.

From time to time, I attend the basketball games of the Chicago Bulls. During breaks in the action, a funny mascot called Benny the Bull emerges onto the court. He's a red, furry character with bull horns who gets the crowd fired up. As a spectator, you feel attached to Benny when he shoots T-shirts into the seats or does backflips on the court. He's like the craziest fan ever. Yet we all know that inside Benny's costume is some fellow who hangs up his suit after the game and goes home to his normal life. That guy is one individual, but he adopts an alter ego during the game. So there are two cooperating personas in Benny the Bull.

But Jesus can't be like that! The Bible doesn't depict the incarnation as the heavenly Son of God cooperating with an earthly man named Jesus inside a single body. Such a schizophrenic approach to Christology will not work. This type of view forced the Antiochian theologians to say some strange things, like "He went into him" and "He operated him." What? Two pronouns? No way. Theologically, there's no "he plus him" in Jesus. The Son of God isn't a two-headed monster with a split personality. The incarnation can't be understood as God operating a human persona, like the guy inside Benny the Bull. Jesus Christ has to be *one, unified person.*

So while the Antiochians did well to preserve the real manhood of Jesus, they didn't quite nail the correct theology. Maybe the Alexandrian church fathers got it right?

Alexandria: City of the Divine Logos

Down in Egypt, the city of Alexandria was the intellectual center of the Roman world. Lofty ideas were constantly being debated there by the empire's leading philosophers. And within the church, the intellectual Christians of Alexandria set their minds on things above. This inclined them to emphasize the deity and unity of Jesus in their Christology.

The Alexandrians liked to use the language of John's Gospel to describe Jesus. They called him the *logos*, or "Word." He was eternal, glorious, and magnificent! But the Jesus who was weary from a day's travel, or sad enough to weep at the death of a friend, or agonized upon the cross—yeah, not so much. The Alexandrians didn't deny those biblical truths. They just set the weakness of Jesus off to the side, which meant his full humanity wasn't functionally a part of their Christology.

The Alexandrians often talked about the "flesh" of Jesus. In and of itself, there's nothing wrong with that. John 1:14 says, "The Word (*logos*) became flesh and made his dwelling among us." Yet for the Alexandrians, the glorious deity of Christ was so preeminent that it seemed as if his flesh was just an outer coating—like a cake that's already delicious, but then it gets some chocolate icing to make it even better. The "real thing" is the cake, whether or not it has any icing on the outside. Is Jesus' manhood nothing but an external wrap?

When the Alexandrians went on and on about the heavenly *logos*, the theologians up in Antioch began to wonder, "Have our Egyptian brothers forgotten Jesus of Nazareth, the carpenter who walked the dusty roads of Galilee? Is this *logos* of theirs just a celestial deity with an outer coating of flesh—or is he really, truly a man?" The Antiochians wanted to include true manhood along with the *logos*.

Neither side completely denied the other's point of view. Yet like our theological debates today, the people who insisted on *A* couldn't find room to acknowledge the full truth of *B*—and vice versa. The ancient church in the fifth century was divided over Christology. So, just like at Nicaea in the fourth century, it was time once again for the Christians to meet together and figure this one out.

The Council of Chalcedon

In the year 451, a great convocation of bishops gathered at Chalcedon, which is today a suburb of Istanbul, Turkey. Their debates were far too intricate for me to describe here. Instead, I will skip straight to the final outcome: The doctrine of hypostatic union. The Greek word *hypostasis* means a "person," and of course, union refers to oneness. So the church decided at Chalcedon to emphasize the view that Jesus is *one person*. You can almost hear the cheers of the Alexandrians as they cried, "Yes! That's what we've been saying! The *logos* took on flesh, but he always remained one person!" No Benny the Bull schizophrenia was allowed at Chalcedon. The unity of Christ was preserved.

But what about the twoness of Jesus? Aren't we supposed to think of him as the God-Man? Indeed we are, so the ancient Christians used a different word. They declared that Christ has *two natures*. This made the Antiochians happy, for they knew there had to be some kind of duality in Jesus (though their split-personality thing wasn't the right way to describe it). The word *nature* didn't imply separate persons in Christ, but rather two equally important aspects: a fully divine nature and a fully human one. This isn't a 50-50 split. Jesus is 100 percent human and 100 percent divine. Even today, we still use the word *nature* to describe that twofold reality.

At Chalcedon, the doctrine of hypostatic union was expressed in a creed that the council produced. Today we call it the Chalcedonian Definition. It declares,

> Following the holy fathers, we teach with one voice that the Son of God and our Lord Jesus Christ is to be confessed as one and the same Person, that he is perfect in Godhead and perfect in manhood, *truly God* and *truly man*...[He] must be confessed to be *in two natures*, unconfusedly, immutably, indivisibly, inseparably united, without the distinction of natures being taken away by such *union*...not separated or divided into two persons, but *one and the same* Son and only-begotten, God the Word, our Lord Jesus Christ.[1]

Can you see the delicate balance that was achieved here? The council fathers got it exactly right! Jesus is a single, unified person who is fully

---

1. *Nicene and Post-Nicene Fathers*, Second Series, vol. 14, pp. 264–65, emphasis added.

human and fully divine. Although these natures of his are distinct, he isn't split in two beings or divided into two personalities. He is the one Son of God, our beloved Savior, Jesus Christ.

Crossing the Divide

My friends, is this ancient creed just a bunch of wrangling over trivialities? Does all this really matter? Perhaps you might think this perfect balance of two views makes no practical difference in your life. If so, I ask you to bring a simple image to your mind.

Think of your sin as an eternal pit into which you might fall. Then, the next time you're about to drive over a bridge, think back on this chapter. As your car zooms onto the bridge, you can decide for yourself whether a perfect balance of opposite ends really does matter to your life!

In Christ all the fullness of the Deity lives in bodily form.

COLOSSIANS 2:9

25

Every Church Must Have an Elevator

In the city of Chicago where I work, and to which I have commuted for many years, there is a 100-story skyscraper known as the John Hancock Center. Chicago has many tall buildings, of course, but the Hancock Center is one of the tallest and is close to my workplace. When you approach this building, you are in a busy shopping district. The Magnificent Mile is nearby, with all its upscale stores drawing lots of shoppers and tourists. Buses rumble past, cab drivers honk their horns, traffic cops blow their whistles, and pedestrians talk on their phones. From every direction, you're assaulted by the loud clamor of a big city.

But then you enter the Hancock Center and notify the attendant that you have dinner reservations at the Signature Room. You step into an elevator and the doors close off the sounds of the Windy City. After a remarkably long time—the restaurant is on the 95th floor—the doors open again. You step out...and everything has changed. Gone is the hustle and bustle of the street. In an atmosphere of quiet elegance, you are shown to your table. To the west, the sun is setting over the distant Illinois prairie. To the east lies the vast blue expanse of Lake Michigan. All around you are the skyscrapers of Chicago—most of them below you, except for a few tall brethren at eye level. Even the clouds are often below you. At 1,054 feet above the urban landscape, you feel like you've entered another world. For the next hour or so, you'll be a citizen of the sky.

My hope in this chapter is that you'll come to believe that every church must have an elevator. Of course, I'm not talking about opening a luxury restaurant high above the sanctuary so the pastor can entertain his fancy guests. Nor am I talking about installing a passenger elevator so the infirm can move between floors (though that's not a bad idea). No, I'm speaking metaphorically. Every church needs the elevator of *worship*—for the purpose of worship is to lift the congregation into the presence of the Lord. When people come to church, they should believe they've ascended to the forecourt of heaven. The ancient church understood this truth, and that's why they developed a liturgical and musical tradition that would elevate worshipers from the muck and mire of earth to the glorious throne room of God.

A Public Work

Ancient church services were structured around a *liturgy*. What does this word mean? Originally, *leitourgia* had nothing to do with churches. It referred to a "public work" that rich citizens provided for the common people, such as festivals, athletic games, or necessary army equipment. But since the worship of the gods was also viewed as valuable for the public well-being, *leitourgia* included the idea of priestly service on the citizens' behalf.

The Bible uses the word *leitourgia* to describe the ministry of the Jewish priesthood in Jerusalem. In Luke 1:5-25, we read that John the Baptist's father, the priest Zechariah, was called to the temple to minister before the Lord. Verse 23 says, "When the days of his priestly service [*leitourgia*] were ended, he went back home" (NASB). This Greek word is even used to describe the ministry of our Lord himself. Instead of the Old Testament "ministry" of bloody sacrifices (Hebrews 9:21), our great High Priest "has obtained a more excellent ministry" (Hebrews 8:6 NASB). A liturgy, then, is a work that benefits God's people. It isn't some kind of dead ritual as some Christians suspect. Properly understood, a liturgy is nothing less than a public enactment of the greatest truths the world could ever know.

In the liturgy of the Christian church, human beings catch a glimpse of what heavenly worship is all about. Though our bodies stay down here on earth, our souls are lifted before the divine presence and our spiritual eyes see spiritual things. That is why liturgy is a public service. It does something beautiful for the sake of the world. The truths enacted in a liturgy are so sublime, so magnificent, so truly *true*, that the church must declare them in a public way. Christians can do nothing less than shout these great truths into the cosmos. And like Jesus said, "if they keep quiet, the stones will cry out" (Luke 19:40). May we never be silent about these glorious things! Liturgy exists to invite all humankind to ride the church's elevator into the very throne room of God.

The Shape of the Liturgy

Although the ancient church's liturgy evolved over time, it always had a certain basic shape. This was because the churches drew from the practices of Jewish worship, which included:

- Exclamations of praise and thanksgiving ("Blessed be the Lord forever! Amen and Amen" Psalm 89:52 NASB)

- Recitation of a "creed" (the Shema, Deuteronomy 6:4)

- Priestly blessings ("The Lord bless you and keep you; the Lord make his face shine on you…" Numbers 6:24-26)

- Readings of Scripture, with exhortations (like Jesus did in Luke 4:14-21; see also Acts 13:15)

- Hymn singing or chanting (more on that in a moment)

- Meal liturgies (such as the Passover Seder, which is what the Last Supper was)

All these Jewish observances had counterparts in ancient Christian worship. We have ample evidence for each of them. The practices of

202 ◆ WISDOM from the ANCIENTS

Judaism gave a basic coherence and structure to the liturgy of the early Christians.

Over time, the worship practices of the ancient church became more standardized and ritualized, especially as Christians began to meet in dedicated church buildings (see the next chapter for that). Although it's tempting to view this as a downfall from a happy, free, and relaxed meeting to one that's rigid, dead, and rote, that perspective isn't accurate at all (and it probably says something about our own culture's informality that we so quickly want to think that way). The reality is, the synagogue was highly structured, and so were early house churches. Although a layer of ritual and fixed wording was added over time, the same basic things were being done throughout the ancient church era.

We have an excellent summary from Justin Martyr of what took place during a second-century church service. He describes the Christian gathering this way:

> On the day called Sunday, all who live in cities or in the country gather together to one place, and the memoirs of the apostles or the writings of the prophets are read,[1] as long as time permits. Then, when the reader has ceased, the leader verbally instructs and exhorts everyone to the imitation of these good things. Then we all rise together and pray. And when our prayer is ended, bread and wine and water are brought, and the leader in like manner offers prayers and thanksgivings, according to his ability. And the people assent, saying, "Amen"…And [after communion] those who are well off, and willing, give what each thinks fit; and what is collected is deposited with the leader, who aids the orphans and widows and those who, through sickness or any other cause, are in need, and those who are in chains, and the strangers sojourning among us. And so he takes care of all who are in need.[2]

What do we learn from this description of ancient Christian worship?

---

1. This seems to be how Justin describes what we know as the New and Old Testaments.

2. *First Apology* 67.

Whether it was in a more casual setting like this one or the more ritualized version that came soon after, we see the same liturgical elements: Scripture reading, pastoral instruction and exhortation, corporate prayer, the Lord's Supper, thanksgiving, and the collection of a charitable offering. These are the basic things Christians still do today. Truly, the work of the church is for the benefit of the whole world.

Psalms, Hymns, and Spiritual Songs

If you are one of those people who loves a good hymn or worship chorus, perhaps you're wondering why Justin didn't mention singing in the summary above. Though I'm not sure why he omitted it there, I can tell you that he did mention hymn singing earlier in the same work.[3] This practice was so common that when one persecuting Roman governor arrested some Christians and inquired about what they did in their secret services, he learned that they "sing a hymn responsively between themselves, to Christ, as if to a god."[4] This evidence fits with the apostle Paul's command that Christians should "[speak] to one another with psalms, hymns, and songs from the Spirit. Sing and make music from your heart to the Lord" (Ephesians 5:19; see also Colossians 3:16).

Notice that the only kind of music mentioned here is singing. Although modern people may find this strange, the ancient Christians were opposed to all forms of instrumental music. This resistance lasted for the first 800 years of church history until the pipe organ was introduced to church worship in medieval times. The reason the ancients detested instrumental music was its association with evil practices: pagan temple worship, the bawdy shows of the theater or circus, and debauched banquets and orgies. Though we can appreciate their moral reservations, nonetheless, I think this is a place where the ancients were not wise. Musical instruments can be redeemed from wicked uses for the glory of God (Psalm 33:3).

---

3. *First Apology* 13.

4. Pliny the Younger, *Epistle* 10.96.7.

Yet when it came to vocal music, the ancient Christians were enthusiastic early adopters. Church services normally included the chanting of Scripture, not only the psalms of Israel but selections from throughout the Bible and other prayerful words. In the fourth century and beyond, formal responsive singing became common. A leader called a *cantor* would sing portions of the service, and the congregation would respond with a refrain at the right time. Antiphonal singing involved two groups singing portions of the Psalms back and forth with each other. This practice was adopted especially by monks, leading to the hauntingly beautiful music known as Gregorian chant in Latin, or Byzantine chant in Greek.

Choirs were also an important part of ancient worship. In the early second century, Ignatius of Antioch said a choir symbolizes Christian unity: "Therefore, in your concord and harmonious love, Jesus Christ is sung…Become a choir, so that by being harmonious in love, and taking up the song of God in unison, you may with one voice sing to the Father through Jesus Christ."[5] Another church father, Ephrem the Syrian, was so devoted to choirs and hymn-writing that he became known as the Harp of the Holy Spirit. Ephrem formed choirs not only of men, but also of sacred virgins. In this way, the voices of women, who could not preach in church, would be able to edify God's people.

One of the earliest Christians hymns—with lyrics so worshipful it is still often sung today—is the *Phos Hilaron*. This is an evening hymn for the time when lamps are lit in honor of the Light of the world. We do not know the composer of this song, but whoever it was understood worship in spirit and in truth. The words are:

> O gracious light, pure brightness of the
>   everliving Father in heaven,
> O Jesus Christ, holy and blessed!
> Now as we come to the setting of the sun,
> and our eyes behold the vesper light,
>   we sing your praises, O God: Father, Son,
>   and Holy Spirit.

---

5. *Epistle to the Ephesians* 4.

You are worthy at all times to be praised by happy voices,
O Son of God, O Giver of Life,
and to be glorified through all the worlds.[6]

When the disciples sang a hymn at the conclusion of the Last Supper and went out at dusk to the garden of Gethsemane (Matthew 26:30), their song certainly wasn't the *Phos Hilaron*. Even so, its holy ardor and profound truths would have been entirely appropriate for that moment!

The Forecourt of Heaven

In the Old Testament temple, the holy of holies was the place where God's presence dwelled. It was surrounded by outer courts where only certain people could go. Today, of course, the Spirit of God lives in believers, who form a new temple (1 Corinthians 3:16). God now dwells nearby. Yet there is another sense in which the full glory of God's presence isn't yet revealed to us. Only through the liturgy and hymnody of the church do we earth-bound mortals get a glimpse of the splendor above. We are transported into the forecourt of heaven, peeking into the throne room where we will one day worship for eternity. Revelation 5:11-12 describes the awe-inspiring glory of this place:

> I looked and heard the voice of many angels, numbering thousands upon thousands, and ten thousand times ten thousand. They encircled the throne and the living creatures and the elders. In a loud voice they were saying: "Worthy is the Lamb, who was slain, to receive power and wealth and wisdom and strength and honor and glory and praise!"

It is to such a sublime height that we are elevated when we enter the house of the Lord. The ancients remind us that the goal of a church service isn't just to *exhort*, but to *transport*. So the next time you go to church, don't expect to stay glued to your seat. Instead, press that

---

6. Translation from the Anglican *Book of Common Prayer*.

button for the top floor. And when the doors open again, remember to cover your eyes, for you're in the blazing presence of God.

> *Since, then, you have been raised with Christ, set your hearts*
> *on things above, where Christ is, seated at the right hand of*
> *God. Set your minds on things above, not on earthly things.*
>
> Colossians 3:1-2

26

Jesus' Head Needs
a Lot More Oil

The titles *Messiah* (from Hebrew) and *Christ* (from Greek) were rightly applied to Jesus of Nazareth. Both of these words mean "anointed one," and they speak of an anointing with olive oil that symbolizes God's favor and empowerment. But can you think of a time when Jesus was actually anointed with oil?

Yes, it did happen. Surprisingly, though, it wasn't a great prophet, a fellow king, or any man at all who anointed God's Messiah. It was a mere woman—someone who, in those days, would have ranked lower than men when it came to such things. This humble anointer was Mary of Bethany, the same woman who sat at Jesus' feet while Martha was busy and who saw her brother Lazarus raised from the dead (John 11:2; 12:3; Luke 10:39). When Mary broke open her alabaster jar of oil and poured it on Jesus' head and feet, she made him, in a literal sense, the Anointed One. Ironically, the Messiah's anointing was actually a preparation for his burial. The king of the universe was about to embark on the road to the cross.

Three of the four Gospel writers tell this story, and each of them emphasizes how costly the ointment was. Matthew and Mark call it "very expensive perfume" (Matthew 26:7; Mark 14:3) and John says it cost 300 denarii (John 12:5). In Bible times, a denarius was a day's wage.

Since Jews didn't work on the Sabbath, that leaves 312 workdays in a year, so 300 denarii would be roughly equivalent to a common worker's annual income. How much would that be today? According to the US Bureau of Labor Statistics, the mean annual wage for a construction laborer is about $40,000. So when Mary poured that jar of ointment on Jesus' head, she was, in effect, giving him something equivalent to what a well-equipped SUV would cost in our times.

But unlike the gift of a vehicle, which has ongoing use, the perfume in this story was used up right away. It's as if the donated SUV could only be driven for one day, then it was gone forever. You would probably consider that wasteful—and so did some of the observers of this lavish gift, who said the money would have been better used to serve the poor. These naysayers were led by the crafty Judas Iscariot, who actually wanted to pilfer the moneybag (John 12:6).

Jesus, however, had low regard for such thinking. He sharply rebuked those who criticized Mary.

> "Leave her alone," said Jesus. "Why are you bothering her? She has done a beautiful thing to me. The poor you will always have with you, and you can help them any time you want. But you will not always have me. She did what she could. She poured perfume on my body beforehand to prepare for my burial. Truly I tell you, wherever the gospel is preached throughout the world, what she has done will also be told, in memory of her" (Mark 14:6-9).

Ever since that day, people have marveled at the lavish love displayed by Mary of Bethany.

How might we show such love for Jesus today? Clearly, serving the poor is one way. The Christian church has a calling to "do good to all people, especially to those who belong to the family of believers" (Galatians 6:10). But so long as that duty is not shirked, other forms of "oil" can be lavished upon our Savior's head as well. Such expenditures are not wasteful but worshipful, for he is worthy of all we can give.

This chapter will look at two interrelated topics: Early Christian art and architecture. Both are concerned with beauty. Yet beauty comes at a cost. Should we always choose cheap drabness so we can save money for more "practical" purposes? The church fathers didn't think so. Their mission wasn't just to meet human needs but also to make beauty in this world. The ancients understood that beauty is just as much a human need as food and shelter. God the Creator made a beautiful world, so we reflect his divine image when we become beauty makers for his everlasting praise and glory.

The Beginnings of Christian Art

Many of the world's most splendid artworks, such as Michelangelo's *David* or the ceiling of the Sistine Chapel, emerged from within the Christian tradition. Yet Christian art had an inauspicious starting point: the dark, underground tunnels of the catacombs. It was here that the early Christians began to bury their dead in the late second century. The gravediggers were organized into teams that included painters. On the walls between the sealed niches for the corpses, the Christians represented their belief that death would not have the final word. The underworld couldn't hold the believer in Jesus forever. One day, the trumpet would sound. Then the dead in Christ would rise!

We have already learned in this book's opening chapter how the concept of resurrection was illustrated by the church fathers: through the Jonah story. A common sequence depicted in early Christian art was Jonah being engulfed by the monstrous creature of the abyss; then bursting forth in triumph; then resting under the vines of paradise. This three-act story portrayed the glorious promise of the Christian's escape from Satan's ravenous maw.

Another common resurrection motif portrayed in catacomb art was Lazarus, still wrapped in his grave clothes, yet emerging from his tomb at a simple command from his Lord. In that miracle, it wasn't Mary but Martha who received the Anointed One's promise: "'I am the resurrection and the life. The one who believes in me will live, even though they die; and whoever lives by believing in me will never die. Do you believe this?' 'Yes, Lord,' she replied, 'I believe that you are the Messiah, the Son of God, who is to come into the world'" (John 11:25-27). With those words, Jesus brought the brother of Mary and Martha back from the grave. What a triumphant story this is! I like to think that many ancient Christians touched the pictures of Lazarus as they buried their loved ones in the catacombs with tears on their cheeks but resurrection hope in their hearts.

Art After Constantine

With the rise of Constantine and all the emperors after him, imperial support and funds were available for creating Christian art. This led to a blossoming of beautiful mosaics in churches across the empire. Even today, many of these stunning artworks have survived. For example, the city of Ravenna, Italy, is a UNESCO World Heritage Site because of them. The churches and baptisteries there look just as dazzling now as they did in the sixth century!

In the post-Constantinian period, artists started depicting Jesus more frequently. Prior to that, he was commonly portrayed by abstract symbols, such as a lamb, a loaf, or a fish. Why a fish? The Greek letters of the word *ichthus* formed an acrostic for the phrase, "Jesus Christ, the Son of God, the Savior."[1] Sometime in the third century, Christians also began to depict Jesus as a youth with curly hair and no beard, holding a sheep over his shoulders. In this way they borrowed the artistic imagery of the god Hermes and turned it into the biblical concept of the Good Shepherd (John 10:11; Hebrews 13:20; 1 Peter 2:25). Another example of repurposing pagan artistic themes for Christian use was to give Jesus the attributes of a sun god, such as shining rays bursting from his head. This was because Jesus overcame death at dawn on Easter, and he is called the "sun of righteousness" in Malachi 4:2 (see also John 8:12).

After the third century, when portraits of Jesus became more widespread, he began to be depicted in the familiar way we know today: as a dark-haired, bearded man with a thin face and piercing eyes. Some

---

1. Augustine, *City of God* 18.23. I have heard modern Christians say that the ancients used to recognize each other by drawing two arcs to make a "Christian fish" sign, but no such thing was ever mentioned by the early church writers.

of the most beautiful mosaics and frescos from the Greek East portray him as the *Pantocrator*—Christ the Almighty (Revelation 1:8). In these depictions, a front-facing Jesus is shown seated on a throne in a high area such as a church dome, reminding the believers down below that the Lord reigns in heaven and surveys the whole earth under his watchful eye.

At the end of the ancient period and into the historical era called Byzantine, some Eastern Christians began to venerate portraits of Christ or the saints called icons. Usually these images were painted onto wooden panels. While I can appreciate the reverence felt toward anything that reminds us of our holy Lord or the great Christians who followed him, we should be careful not to let that respect get anywhere close to worship of the picture itself.

From Houses to Basilicas

What about Christian buildings? The earliest generations of Christians met in everyday spaces—not just houses but shops, gardens, banquet venues, warehouses, and even bathhouses for baptisms. The ancient believers rejected the idea that you had to go to a specific temple and find an idol in order to reach a god. Since the true God is everywhere, any building can be a house of worship.

But by the late third century, the number of Christian converts had grown to the point that casual spaces couldn't work anymore. The size of the congregations required bigger rooms, and space was also needed to store church valuables and items to be given out in charity. Some bishops began purchasing houses for permanent Christian use. A few pioneering bishops even constructed special worship halls. But it was Constantine's rise to power that really began the tradition of Christian architecture. He patronized a church-building program across the empire. Yet this raised an interesting question: What kind of architecture should a church have?

Over the course of the next few centuries, the whole apparatus of pagan temples was dismantled. Sometimes these buildings were turned into churches instead. But there was a problem with this. Even after the place had been cleansed of its idolatrous connections, it still didn't fit well with Christianity. Pagans went to temples not for fellowship but to coerce the idol with an offering. So there wasn't a lot of room inside a temple—it was just a roof over the god's head. Therefore, the Christians turned instead to an existing architectural form that was perfect for large gatherings: the basilica.

Most Greek and Roman towns had a basilica on the main square. It was a royal hall, a place for seeking justice and conducting public business. The early Christians adopted this architectural form but put it to a much different use. Basilicas had *aisles* on either side where men and women could worship separately. They had a central *nave* lit by high windows where clergy could proceed in for the service. And they had a curved area at the far end of the hall known as the *apse* where the bishop could sit to preach from his chair called a *cathedra*—the origin of our word, *cathedral*. The altar for communion would also be in or near the apse. Now the Christian church was ready for its style of worship in the next millennium and beyond.

Heavenly Beauty on Earth

In a medieval text called the *Book of the Popes* we have a record of what Emperor Constantine donated to Bishop Sylvester of Rome. For serving communion, the imperial gifts included silver dishes, goblets, pitchers, and even a two-pound chalice made of gold. For lighting the basilica, we read of 20 chandeliers, 40 oil lamps, and 24 bronze candelabras weighing 30 pounds each.

Can you imagine going to church in a place like this on some wintry Roman evening? The light from these many flames would sparkle around you like the stars. The glittering mosaics on the walls would dazzle your eyes and humble your heart. The marble tiles on the floor would please your sense of color and proportion with their intricate geometric patterns. The beautiful tableware would invite you to the heavenly feast. And high above, Jesus the Almighty would gaze down upon you—approving of your love for him, yet also stern-faced in the holiness of his righteous demands.

Please understand: I'm not saying that Jesus isn't equally present in a thatched hut, an open-air meadow, or a rented school gymnasium. Our Lord can be met anywhere, and I celebrate that! Yet what I *am* suggesting is that we are made by God to respond to beauty—as well as to create beauty around us. This is part of our noble calling as image-bearers.

The highest purpose for human artistic endeavors isn't to populate museums or make big money at art auctions. It is to adorn the Christian faith so the infinite beauty of Jesus might be glimpsed here on earth. That is what Mary of Bethany understood. She poured that oil upon Jesus' head because only a short time earlier, her beautiful Savior had called forth her brother from the grave. And so too, Jesus is our Resurrection and Life. Doesn't this great truth demand a response from us—the utmost beauty we can give? Properly understood, Christian art isn't about waste. It's about lavish love for the one who is truly worthy.

One thing I ask from the LORD, this only do I seek:
that I may dwell in the house of the LORD all the days of my life,
to gaze on the beauty of the LORD and to seek him in his temple.

PSALM 27:4

27

Every Christian Is a Witness, but Not Every Christian Is a Missionary

One of the things you often hear Christians say is that we're all on a mission. Believers have joined a mission to save the world. We're supposed to engage in missional living. As the Blues Brothers put it—those insightful theologians with the nasal Chicago accents from the 1980 movie—"We're on a mission from *Gahd.*"

At a basic level, this is true. Christians are, indeed, on a mission from God. The word *mission* comes from a Latin verb that means "to send out." And Jesus did send us out. In Matthew 28:19-20, he told his followers to "go and make disciples of all nations, baptizing them in the name of the Father and of the Son and of the Holy Spirit, and teaching them to obey everything I have commanded you." None of us is exempt from this Great Commission.

Yet that doesn't mean we're all missionaries. For that word to mean anything, it can't just be equivalent to "a Christian." Though all of us evangelize, not all of us "go into all the world and preach the gospel to all creation" (Mark 16:15). Some Christians evangelize by staying. Others evangelize by going. And we fail to honor the courage of those who cross difficult boundaries when we apply the word *mission* to us all. Our missionaries who make exceptional sacrifices deserve to be honored as a distinct group. Let's give missionaries their rightful due—not so we can idolize them, but so we can glorify the God who equipped and empowered them for their high calling.

The ancient church understood that every Christian is called to be a *witness*, but not everyone is called to be a *missionary*. Those words mean two different things, and only the second one has the connotation of being sent somewhere else. Consider how the church historian Eusebius celebrated the work of the missionaries who

> built up the foundations of the churches which had been laid by the apostles in every place, and preached the Gospel even more widely, and scattered the saving seeds of the kingdom of heaven far and near throughout the whole world…Then starting out upon long journeys they performed the office of evangelists, being filled with the desire to preach Christ to those who had not yet heard the word of faith, and to deliver to them the divine Gospels. And when they had laid the foundations of the faith in foreign places, they appointed others as pastors, and entrusted them with the nurture of those that had recently been brought in, while they themselves went on again to other countries and nations, with the grace and assistance of God. For a great many wonderful works were done through them by the power of the divine Spirit, so that at the first hearing [of the Gospel], whole multitudes of men eagerly embraced the religion of the Creator of the universe.[1]

In this chapter, we'll meet some missionaries like the ones Eusebius so eloquently described. We'll also learn what it means to be witnesses for God—a Christian duty that sometimes comes at a cost. Yet witness we must, for the gospel is good news for the whole world.

"Eyewitnesses of His Majesty"

The apostle Peter witnessed some amazing things in his lifetime. Like what? His feet standing firm upon water (at least for a moment).

---

1. *Church History* 3.37.1–3.

Miraculous catches of fish. Healings of the blind and the lame. The shining glory of Jesus on a mountain top. The empty tomb with the grave clothes laid aside. The risen Christ ascending to heaven. The Holy Spirit falling like tongues of fire. And the salvation of thousands of souls. Truly, Peter was speaking from firsthand experience when he said, "We did not follow cleverly devised stories when we told you about the coming of our Lord Jesus Christ in power, but we were eyewitnesses of his majesty" (2 Peter 1:16).

It is because Peter saw the risen Lord that he can be called an apostle. This word refers to those who were sent out by Jesus to bear witness to what they had seen with their own two eyes. Only the first generation of Christians could be apostles, for only they had witnessed Jesus after the resurrection. The apostle John put it this way: "That which was from the beginning, which we have heard, which we have seen with our eyes, which we have looked at and our hands have touched—this we proclaim concerning the Word of life" (1 John 1:1).

As time went on, the generation of the eyewitness apostles passed. Yet other faithful believers picked up where they left off. These church fathers and mothers hadn't seen Jesus with their own eyes. Yet they had spoken with those who did. They had received the apostolic testimony. And of course, they had seen Jesus' power in their lives. Although they couldn't bear witness to the nail holes in the Savior's hands, they could still testify to what their Lord had done for them. In this way, as Christian travelers proclaimed their encounter with Jesus wherever they went, the church began to grow.

Beyond verbal evangelism, how else did the church grow? As we learned back in chapter 2, "Weakness is the best witness." One of the ancient church's most powerful evangelistic tools was martyrdom. The word *martyr* means "witness." When people die for what they believe, they bear witness that their faith can withstand the ultimate test. Martyr stories abound with examples of pagans who came to believe in Jesus because of a Christian's courage—like Pudens who received a gold ring dipped in the blood of Saturus after he was mauled by a leopard. Whenever a martyr's blood is sown in the sand of the arena, you can bet that an abundant harvest of salvation is about to be reaped.

218 ◆ WISDOM from the ANCIENTS

From Witnesses to Missionaries

The earliest missionary movements usually stayed within the Roman Empire. When we consider how vast the empire was, how difficult it was to travel within it, and how utterly pagan it was from the Atlantic Ocean to the Euphrates River, we gain a sense of the daunting task that faced the ancient church. Even so, some roving evangelists took up the challenge. Soon, the cities of the empire were gaining churches like a series of candles being lit from the original flame. When the tongues of fire came upon the disciples in the upper room, it was a foretaste of great things to come.

Many ancient legends say that the 12 apostles went to the far corners of the earth. While this isn't true—or at least, we don't know for sure what all of them did—we do have good evidence that at least some of them went very far away.[2] One example is the apostle Thomas. This disciple of Jesus is famous for doubting, but he was actually a great man of faith who was willing to die with his Lord (John 11:16). We have solid reasons to believe that Thomas traveled eastward from Jerusalem at least as far as Edessa, which was located in a foreign land called Osroene. From there, he may have traveled to the land we know today as Pakistan, along the Indus River. He also may have gone to the Malabar Coast of southern India, where many Christians today still venerate his memory. These plausible—though not absolutely certain—legends about Thomas remind us that from the beginning, the ancient church possessed a cross-cultural missionary impulse.

By the fourth century, changes in the structure of the ancient church allowed Christians to tackle even bigger missionary endeavors. A system was put into place in which the whole empire was divided into "dioceses" where bishops would have the responsibility of evangelizing their local region. One example of this process was a monk named Martin who in AD 372 became bishop of Tours in France. Martin realized that while the city dwellers had a chance to hear the gospel from established churches, the country folk were still resolutely

---

2. To sort out what we can actually believe about the work of the apostles and what is probably just pious fiction, see my book *After Acts: Exploring the Lives and Legends of the Apostles* (Moody, 2015).

pagan. So Martin initiated the strategy of establishing monasteries as evangelistic bases in the countryside and traveling regularly to meet with the common people. When the peasantry saw their bishop's holy life and realized how he loved them, they left the old gods in droves and converted to faith in Christ. Martin of Tours was an effective evangelist of the ancient church.

Sometimes, God moves the nations to places where they can hear the gospel instead of sending missionaries to them. This happened to the wandering Germanic people called the Franks who settled in the area that now bears their name: France. None of them were Christians when they first arrived. They had gods such as Odin and Thor. But then God used an unexpected person to convert King Clovis of the Franks to Christianity: his pious and godly wife, Queen Clotilda.

At first, when Clotilda bore witness about Jesus, her husband scoffed at her. For several years, this mockery continued. But then the day came in the year 496 when Clovis found himself losing a great battle. Desperate for divine help, he prayed to his wife's God with these words: "Jesus Christ, whom Clotilda asserts to be the son of the living God, who are said to give aid to those in distress and to bestow victory on those who hope in thee, I request the glory of thy aid, with the vow that if thou will grant me victory over these enemies...I will believe in thee and be baptized in thy name."[3] Admittedly, this isn't the typical sinner's prayer! Yet this was how ancient pagan warriors came to believe in Christ. Clovis went on to win the battle, get baptized, and establish a mighty Frankish kingdom with Paris as its capital. Was it a true conversion? Hard to say. But at least now the name of Jesus was being proclaimed across France instead of the bloody gods of war.

Missionary to the Irish

Although many of the pagan peoples of northern Europe wandered into the Roman Empire and encountered Christianity there, not all of them did. One place that remained largely untouched by the

---

3. Gregory of Tours, *History of the Franks* 2.30.

gospel was Ireland. But do you recall the story of Patrick, whom we met back in chapter 15? While he was just a teenager on Britain's western coast, he was abducted by Irish raiders and taken away as a slave. On that lonely, green island beside the endless Atlantic Ocean, the captive youth rediscovered his faith in Christ. He started saying a hundred prayers every day and night. And as he prayed, the Holy Spirit whispered back to Patrick that God had not forgotten him.

When Patrick finally escaped from his oppressors, he returned to Britain. Things seemed normal again. Yet Patrick recounts that a man appeared to him in a dream and gave him a letter called "The Cry of the Irish." As he read it, Patrick could hear his former captors saying, "We beseech you, holy boy, to come and walk in our midst again."[4] When he woke up, he realized the Lord had called him to live among the Irish for the rest of his life.

Returning to the people who had once enslaved him, Patrick bravely bore witness to the gospel. His words took root in the hearts of the Irish people, and soon many had converted to God. By the time he died around the year 460, Ireland had been widely Christianized—all because God had lit the bonfire of his love in the heart of a teenaged slave.

Near and Far

Whether we labor nearby or far away, an earnest desire for evangelism marks every heart touched by the gospel. Some of us are called to do it locally, like Martin evangelizing the peasantry around Tours, or Queen Clotilda naming Jesus to her warrior husband. Others are called to cross lands and seas, like Paul going to Rome and Spain, Thomas going to India, or Patrick going to Ireland. These folks have a special *missio*, a "sending," from God and their church. Their burdens are greater than most of us are asked to bear: the loss of family relations, the meager income, the difficulty of learning foreign languages, and the strangeness of living in a distant land.

---

4. Patrick, *Confession* 23.

The Christian church is greatly indebted to its missionaries from ancient times to the present. It is these brave boundary crossers who bring the good news of Jesus to ears that haven't yet heard it. Others of us are called to stay rooted like an oak tree and to drop our acorns within the reach of our branches. Together, as we all do our part, the seeds of the gospel will fall on the good soil that God has prepared, yielding a harvest of souls that will last into eternity.

All the ends of the earth will remember and turn to the LORD,
and all the families of the nations will bow down before him.

PSALM 22:27

28

It's Better to Shoot
Than to Roll

Proverbs 6:6 tells us to learn wisdom from the ant. Though the industrious ant is presented in Scripture as a remedy for laziness, I'd like to draw a different lesson from the little creature. Imagine an ant who has found himself on a wagon wheel. As the wheel rolls along, the poor insect is periodically immersed in mud and faces the possibility of being crushed to death. Although he eventually emerges into fresh air, he is always subject to the wheel's rolling. It's only a matter of time until he's back in the mud again—maybe this time to his doom.

But imagine a second ant on a different piece of wood. This ant has crawled onto an arrow's shaft just before it was released from the bow. Perched behind the arrowhead, he is now whizzing toward the target at which the archer has aimed. Before, the ant's life was rather dull. Now, it's an exciting ride. He is shooting toward a final destination. And he has become part of the archer's greater purpose.

The pagan culture of the classical world viewed time like a wheel. The Latin goddess Fortune spun her wheel to determine what would befall the human race. Like her Greek counterpart Tyche (or Luck), Fortune was a blind goddess. She stood on a ball that could lurch in any direction. Sometimes, the ball took a good roll and Fortune bestowed gifts from her cornucopia. Other times, blind fate had terrible disasters in store: break a leg, lose a child, fall into financial ruin. The cosmic wheel of fortune was no TV game show. For the ancients, it was real life. Their destiny was thought to be fated in the stars. Perhaps astrologists could examine the zodiac's wheel and tell someone's fortune. But it couldn't be changed. The circle of life just kept turning: Winter followed summer, rags followed riches, and death followed life. What goes around comes around—and like the ant on the wagon wheel, there wasn't much you could do about it.

This pagan outlook wasn't, however, the early Christian view of time. The ancient church held a fundamentally different concept of how time works, illustrated by the arrow flying toward its destination. Although we do experience recurring seasons, of course, time itself isn't cyclical and arbitrary like the wheel of fortune. God's time has purpose and intent. It is marked by a *past* when important events happened in history; a *present* that gives meaning to life right now; and a *future* that will be glorious and redemptive. And most importantly, time has a pivot point that changed everything: the moment when God became flesh and stepped onto the world's stage. After Jesus Christ, nothing would ever be the same again.

The Church Calendar

Today, some churches observe a liturgical calendar as a way of marking sacred time. These Christians might assume that their calendar was in place from the beginning of church history, but the truth is, it evolved over many centuries to become what it is now. Different seasons, fasts, and holidays were observed by ancient Christian communities at various times and places. Although the modern liturgical calendar does indeed have its roots in the early church, it wasn't firmly fixed until much later.

Yet the roots are important! From the beginning, the believers in Jesus had a strong desire to mark time in a distinctly Christian way. Since the Christian view of time was understood as linear—like an arrow moving toward a goal—three important elements had to be expressed in the church's worship. First, there had to be seasons of *anticipation*, which is a future-oriented virtue of patiently waiting for the good things to come. Second, there had to be *commemoration*, which is a backward remembrance of historical events with deep gratitude for what they represent. Finally, there had to be *celebration*, a time in the here and now when feasting and pleasure can express the exuberant joy of God's good blessings. Of course, Christians can't live continuously in these heightened states. The liturgical seasons have to be limited to fixed periods that are separated by ordinary time. Otherwise, we would live in perpetual hyperawareness, and these seasons wouldn't stand out as special.

It was no easy thing for the Christians to reorient their culture's sense of time to the true God. The Romans, of course, already had a calendar, and it was based on the pagan gods. We still see the vestiges of this in our modern calendar, which contains months named for Janus, Mars, Maia, and Juno, as well as the deified caesars Julius and Augustus. Later, during the Middle Ages when the culture of the Germanic tribes had become prominent in Western Europe, some days of the week also took their gods' names: Tiws' Day, Woden's Day, Thor's Day, and Frigg's Day. Yet the old Roman god Saturn kept his name on one day, and so did the god of the sun and the moon. And it is to the day of the sun that we now turn.

The Lord's Day

All four Gospels record that our Lord's resurrection happened on the "first day of the week" (e.g., Mark 16:1-2). This was the day we call Sunday, the day after the Sabbath. Paul instructs Christians to give their offerings on this day, presumably in their weekly gathering, until he can arrive to collect it (1 Corinthians 16:2). We also read in Acts 20:7 that the Christians "broke bread" on that day and heard a sermon from Paul. And the apostle John received his revelation on "the Lord's Day" (Revelation 1:10). So the Bible gives us every reason to think that the early Christians were accustomed to gather on the day of the Lord's resurrection. This hypothesis is supported by ancient texts written soon after the time of the New Testament. The evidence shows that it was very common for Christians to meet on Sunday (although in Jewish-Christian circles, Sabbath observance continued for a time as well).

Some modern Christians may have heard that the day of the sun was chosen so that a pagan celebration of the sun god could be turned into a Christian holiday. But that is not the way the church fathers thought. They were vehemently against the pagan gods. Instead, Justin Martyr explained it like this: "Sunday is the day on which we all hold our common assembly because it is the first day on which God… made the world; and Jesus Christ our Savior rose from the dead on the same day."[1] Justin believed that the first day of the Genesis creation week (Genesis 1:2-5) was also the day of Christ's resurrection. So Sunday was about new beginnings, not pagan gods.

To the extent that solar imagery was applied to Christ in the ancient church, it expressed a desire to show the true meaning of the unbelievers' false worship of the sun. The rich biblical motifs of light, dawn, and sunshine were applied to Jesus, who conquered death at daybreak on Easter morning (Psalm 84:11; Isaiah 60:1-2; Malachi 4:2; Matthew 4:16; Luke 1:78; John 8:12; Ephesians 5:14). No doubt, some less knowledgeable Christians confused their old deities with the new one. But the church fathers warned against this. Tertullian said that while "we devote Sunday to rejoicing," it is "for a far different reason than sun worship."[2] He admits that some people mistakenly "suppose that the sun is the god of the Christians because it is a well-known fact that we pray towards the east, or because we make Sunday a day of festivity."[3] To clarify the confusion, Tertullian totally rejected solar worship. Though Jesus is symbolized by the light of heaven, the sun itself isn't a proper object of veneration.

Yet in both of these texts I just cited, Tertullian asserts that Sunday was a day of Christian rest. In the fourth century, Emperor Constantine made this the official policy for all citizens of the empire, even for soldiers. We learn from the historian Eusebius that "he commanded

---

1. *First Apology* 67.

2. *Apology* 16.

3. *To the Nations* 1.3.

all the subjects of the Roman Empire to observe the Lord's day as a day of rest...in memory, I suppose, of what the Savior of mankind is recorded to have achieved on that day."[4] This practice of resting on Sunday became so engrained in Western culture that it has continued through all of history to today.

Holy Week

While Sunday was important for the Christians because of the resurrection, they didn't forget what had happened on Thursday and Friday. When Jesus broke bread and shared the cup with his disciples, he was declaring that his sacrifice upon the cross the next day would fulfill the place of the Passover lamb whose blood on the doorposts averted divine wrath (Exodus 12:5-7). This is why the apostle Paul could say, "Christ, our Passover lamb, has been sacrificed" (1 Corinthians 5:7; see also 1 Peter 1:19).

The Jews in the time of the early church fasted on Passover and the days near it. According to the ancient church manual called the *Didache*, Christians adopted Wednesdays and Fridays as their fasting days to distinguish themselves from the Jewish fasts on Mondays and Thursdays.[5] Christian fasting was especially important during the week before Easter, and a Good Friday fast was common. In this practice, we have the beginnings of fasting for Lent.[6] In fact, since the earliest Christians were Jews who already fasted for Passover, there was never a time when Christians didn't mark the Easter season with a fast.

How did Lent come to be 40 days in length? This seems to have emerged from the ancient Christian practice of baptizing converts on Easter morning. Just as Jesus fasted for 40 days before starting his ministry (Matthew 4:2), so the new Christians fasted for that amount of time before embarking on their walk with Christ. Eventually, the

---

4. *Life of Constantine* 4.18.

5. *Didache* 8.1. (This word means "teaching." It is pronounced *Did-ock-HEY*.)

6. Our English word *Lent* is related to the word *lengthen*, because it occurred when the days began to lengthen in the spring.

40-day fast before Easter baptisms became a time of spiritual preparation for everyone. It consisted of 6 weeks of fasting, minus the Sundays which were days for celebration. Since 6 x 6 = 36, 4 more days were required to make Jesus' number of 40, which pushed the start of Lent back to a Wednesday.

Perhaps surprisingly to some, the ancient church didn't use ashes on this day. The observance of Ash Wednesday is first attested in AD 960. However, the concept of expressing one's repentance with ashes is biblical (Job 42:6; Daniel 9:3; Luke 10:13).

What Day Was Christ Born?

For the first three centuries of church history, the Christians didn't liturgically observe the birth of Christ (though a few scholars did try to calculate the date out of curiosity). It was only in the fourth century that celebrating the nativity became common. For a while, two specific dates competed for the honor of marking the incarnation. But by the fifth century, a consensus had emerged that the birth of Jesus happened on December 25, while the manifestation of Jesus to the wise men (Epiphany) happened on January 6, as well as his baptism and his water-into-wine miracle at Cana.

As I mentioned above, some modern Christians think the Christmas date was chosen because pagan festivals were melded with Christianity. And indeed, December 25 was the pagan day of the winter solstice and birthday of the Invincible Sun. However, the evidence shows that the early Christians had already chosen December 25 before it became an important solar holiday. Their reasoning sounds strange to us, but it made perfect sense to them: The date of Christ's conception and his death upon the cross were supposed to be miraculously the same: March 25. So if Jesus was conceived on this date in the womb of Mary, he must have been born exactly nine months later on the day we now know as Christmas. Although the Christians reached this conclusion independently of pagan solar worship, even so, the biblical themes of light and sunshine were viewed as beautiful pictures of Christ. Through this imagery, the sun god was defeated by the Light of the world, and pagan holidays were shown to have their true meaning in Jesus instead.

Sacred Time

By celebrating the holidays of Easter, Christmas, and Epiphany (along with the seasons of preparation that preceded them), the ancient church was making a bold, new statement about sacred time. No longer was the *past* centered on the legendary myths of the gods, but on the historical deeds of Christ. No longer was the *present* a dreadful cycle of capricious fate, but the outworking of God's sovereign purposes. And no longer was the *future* a vague and unknowable "beyond," but the climax of history just as God intended it.

At last, time had meaning! It was a divine gift to humanity, not a crushing wheel. Now the question was: *How will you use the precious allotment of time that God has given you?* That vital question is just as relevant for us as it was for the ancient church.

> *Look carefully then how you walk, not as unwise but as wise,*
> *making the best use of the time, because the days are evil.*
>
> EPHESIANS 5:15-16 ESV

29

The Land of Israel Is
Calling to Your Feet

In the last chapter, we saw that Jesus Christ's entrance into the world revolutionized the meaning of time. In this chapter, we'll see how the same thing was true of space—and in particular, the physical space that Jesus himself had inhabited. Israel was already the promised land of God's chosen people. But with the coming of Jesus to a manger in Bethlehem, the tiny Jewish territory gained a new, and indeed ultimate, reason to be known forever after as the Holy Land. This was the land where God himself had walked upon the earth.

Many people today get their mental images of biblical lands from Christian picture books. If you're like me and you grew up in church, you've been seeing these images since you were a child. But even if you came to faith later in life, you've still probably encountered pop culture depictions of Jesus and his disciples. They're always shown in a sandy environment with palm trees and blocky houses. People back then wore sandals and robes with bright-colored sashes. Pro tip: If you ever have to dress like a Bible character for a Christmas play, your best bet for the costume is a white bathrobe and Birkenstocks. If you can add a diagonal towel, so much the better. Now you're decked out in the height of biblical fashion.

The main problem with these mental images isn't their historical inaccuracy. While that is no doubt true, the problem runs deeper.

Picturing Bible lands like this makes us think that ancient Israel was a mythical place. It seems like a fictionalized environment, just a backdrop for pious fables. Like Middle Earth for the hobbits or Hogwarts for the wizards, the places in the Bible can have a make-believe feel to them. In our minds, we know that actual events happened there. Yet somehow, the setting seems detached from reality.

This isn't just a modern problem. The ancient Christians felt it too, and in time, they developed the urge to do something about it. Of course, the Christians who lived in the land of Israel didn't have this dilemma. They could just look around at the sacred places where biblical events had transpired. But remember that the Roman Empire was a huge place. For a convert living in rainy Britain, forested Gaul, or urbanized Rome, the look and feel of Israel was even more distant than it is for us. We can hop on a plane in New York and be in Tel Aviv in 11 hours. But if ancient Christians from the Western empire wanted to visit the Holy Land, they had to invest 11 months or more. Nevertheless, some did. And the reason they did was because the land of Israel always beckons to the feet of God's pilgrims.

The Land Called Holy

My mentor and PhD dissertation supervisor, the eminent church historian Robert L. Wilken, observes in his book *The Land Called Holy*: "Only gradually, after a period when the idea was shunned, did Christians begin to view the land of the Bible as a Christian Holy Land."[1] Why would some ancient Christians "shun" this idea for a time? Wasn't it a biblical concept? Yes, the prophet Zechariah used this term. He comforted the Jewish exiles with the promise that "the LORD will inherit Judah as his portion in the holy land and will again choose Jerusalem" (Zechariah 2:12).

Even so, the earliest generations of Christians were uncomfortable with the idea of a holy land because they didn't believe God was restricted to a single place. Jesus had told the woman at the well, "a time is coming

---

1. Robert L. Wilken, *The Land Called Holy: Palestine in Christian History and Thought* (1992), xiv.

when you will worship the Father neither on this mountain nor in Jerusalem...the true worshipers will worship the Father in the Spirit and in truth" (John 4:21,23). Christians themselves were the temple of God (1 Corinthians 3:16; 6:19; 2 Corinthians 6:16). Wherever they gathered in the name of Jesus, he was in their midst (Matthew 18:20).

Because the early church believed that God could be found in a humble house just as much as the great temple in Jerusalem—whose destruction in AD 70 seemed to validate this very point—the first Christians didn't put much emphasis on the actual city of Jerusalem in Israel. Of course, everyone remembered it was an important place in the book of Acts. James was its leader, and the apostles had used it as their base of operations. Yet soon enough, Jerusalem sort of faded from people's minds. After the apostolic age, it went back to being a minor city with a small Christian congregation. Let's take a look at that historical demotion—then see how Jerusalem burst back into Christian consciousness in the fourth century.

Jehovah, Jesus, and Jupiter

In the time of King David, Jerusalem became the capital of the Israelites. But David wasn't the founder of the city. He captured this hilltop fortress from the Jebusites (2 Samuel 5:6-9). Once he had established a foothold there, he began to notice the next hilltop over, which was being used as a threshing floor where the wind would help separate the wheat from the chaff. David bought this summit and planned to build God's temple on it (1 Chronicles 21:18-30; 22:1). But David's hands were too bloody (1 Chronicles 22:8), so his son Solomon achieved the deed instead (2 Chronicles 3:1). From this holy place, the light of Yahweh (or Jehovah, as he is sometimes called) became a beacon of hope to the world.

In the time of Jesus, a thousand years later, the temple of Solomon was long gone. Now a second temple constructed by King Herod stood on the same location. Today, this area is known as the Temple Mount, and its top is occupied by a Muslim shrine called the Dome of the Rock. But when Jesus walked the streets of Jerusalem, the religion of Islam hadn't yet come into existence. The Jewish temple stood proudly on the Temple Mount, and it remained there through Jesus' earthly lifetime. Then the Romans destroyed it in AD 70.

As bad as that disaster was, it was the year 135 that really ended Jewish presence in their homeland. An uprising caused the Romans to evict the Jews from Judea. The emperor Hadrian not only renamed the province—eliminating any reference to Judaism—he also renamed its former capital city. From that point on, Jerusalem was called Aelia Capitolina, which honored Hadrian's family, the Aelian clan, and the god Jupiter who lived on Rome's Capitoline Hill.

To make matters worse, Hadrian decreed that two pagan temples should be built in religiously significant places. First, a temple to Jupiter was erected right on the Temple Mount, near the spot where the holy of holies once brought God's presence to earth. And second, Hadrian tried to blot out the tomb that the local Christians remembered as Christ's. Considering that this happened only a hundred years after Jesus' resurrection, many old folks at that time could have been shown the tomb by eyewitnesses of the Lord's crucifixion and burial. The local Christians surely knew which tomb had been Jesus'. And it was this very place that Hadrian smothered with a giant heap of fill dirt. Then he paved it to make a flat terrace and built a temple there on its top for the sex goddess Aphrodite (also called Venus). In fact, her disgusting idol was placed directly over the holy tomb.

For the next two hundred years, the tomb of Christ slept quietly beneath the earth. Hadrian died, and so did the many emperors who ruled after him. Each one believed in the traditional gods of Rome. But then came the pivotal emperor whom we've already met, Constantine, who decided that Jesus was the right God to be worshiped. This Christian emperor wanted to put a new emphasis on the Holy Land. And to lead the exploration of Israel's biblical sites, he sent one of the greatest women of church history: his devout mother, Empress Helena.

The Holy Sepulcher

In the year 326, after a long journey from Rome, Empress Helena arrived in Jerusalem on an exploration mission from her son. Among her other goals, Helena hoped to find the lost sepulcher (tomb) of Christ. Legend mixes with reality in this historical moment, making it hard to separate fact from fiction. Yet let's hear the story of the tomb's discovery from Eusebius, a contemporary of these times and the bishop of nearby Caesarea. He tells it like this:

> In days past, it was the endeavor of impious men (or rather let me say, of the whole race of demons through [human] means) to consign to the darkness of oblivion that divine monument of immortality where the radiant angel had descended from heaven and rolled away the stone…This sacred cave, then, certain impious and godless persons had tried to remove entirely from the eyes of men, supposing in their folly that they should be able to obscure the truth…Unhappy men! They were unable to comprehend how impossible it was that their attempt should remain unknown to Him who had been crowned with victory over death…And now [Constantine], acting as he did under the guidance of the divine Spirit, could not consent to see the sacred spot of which we have spoken thus buried…So as soon as the original surface of the ground beneath the covering of earth appeared, immediately, and contrary to all expectation, the venerable and hallowed monument of our Savior's resurrection was discovered. Then, indeed, did this most holy cave present a faithful analogy of [Jesus'] return to life, in that, after lying buried in darkness, it again emerged to light, and provided…a clear and visible proof of the wonders [that had happened there]—a testimony to the resurrection of the Savior clearer than any voice could give.[2]

Though Eusebius's words are pious and flowery, several other ancient texts—as well as modern archaeology—confirm the basic truth of his report. A first-century Jewish tomb exactly like the Bible describes was found directly underneath the Venus temple. Consider what this means. When Hadrian erected the pagan building, he was

---

2. Eusebius, *Life of Constantine* 3.26, 28.

trying to bury Christianity's most holy site. But actually, he was marking it for later generations to dig it up and build a church there!

A church still stands in that place today. It was rebuilt in the Crusader era after Muslim armies destroyed the Constantinian one. The Church of the Holy Sepulcher is visited by more than a million people every year. If you ever have the chance to kneel inside the tomb of Jesus and pray in this sacred space, you will never forget the experience.

"Where These Things Were Preached and Done"

Modern people who make an Israel trip join a long tradition of Christian pilgrimage. One of the first church fathers to take up this goal was Melito, bishop of Sardis. We learned in chapter 22 that the purpose of his trip was to find out which books belonged in the Old Testament canon. Yet more broadly, Melito tells us that he wanted to see with his own eyes "the place where these things were preached and done."[3]

By the fourth century, as Helena began to fill the Holy Land with churches and historical monuments at Constantine's behest, pilgrimage became very popular for Christians who could afford it. We have a record compiled by one traveler from southern France who made the trip in AD 330, recording each stop along the way for those who might want to follow him. Also, a pious lady named Egeria (probably from Spain) made a four-year trip to the Holy Land in the early 380s, and her travel diary has survived to today. By the late fourth century, this sort of pilgrimage had become common. Even the medieval Crusaders—as violent and horrific as they were—can be put in the category of religious pilgrims.

But heading to the Holy Land with a sword in hand wasn't the norm. The real purpose of pilgrimage is spiritual. There's nothing like seeing the places of the Bible firsthand. Although many practices can help you grow in Christ, by no other means can your devotional life be enriched in this particular way—by seeing, smelling, hearing, touching, and even tasting what Israel has to offer.

---

3. Eusebius, *Church History* 4.26.14.

This land which the prophet Zechariah called "holy" is like no other. God's shining glory was literally there in the temple. Then, God in the flesh walked the length of this land. Such an amazing truth has always made Israel compelling for Christians. Whether it's on the back of a donkey or in the cabin of a jetliner, Christian travelers have never stopped coming to see the place "where these things were preached and done." Is anything stopping you from doing the same?

He is not here; he has risen, just as he said.
Come and see the place where he lay.

MATTHEW 28:6

30

Your Passport Has a Huge Error

One of the most valuable documents a person can own is a United States passport. This little blue booklet opens the world to its owner. Most nations are willing to admit anyone who can show it at the airport or border crossing. On the data page of mine, it says, "Nationality: United States of America." But this is incorrect. As a Christian, my true citizenship is in the kingdom of heaven. My passport should actually say, "The City of God."

Where exactly is this city? In the previous chapter, we saw how the ancient Christians paid little attention to Jerusalem at first, but eventually rediscovered it in the fourth century. This initial neglect was due in part to Scripture's teaching about the heavenly city to which we belong instead of an earthly one. Hebrews 12:22-23 vividly describes our future destiny: "You have come to Mount Zion, to the city of the living God, the heavenly Jerusalem. You have come to thousands upon thousands of angels in joyful assembly, to the church of the firstborn, whose names are written in heaven. You have come to God, the Judge of all." The apostle Paul puts it more succinctly: "The Jerusalem above is free, and she is our mother" (Galatians 4:26 ESV). To be a Christian is to have a celestial citizenship reserved for us at the end of time. Nothing is more hopeful than knowing our Savior will one day welcome us to our eternal home.

Most people in the Roman Empire didn't have such a secure hope. They believed that the souls of the dead formed a kind of shadowy group in the underworld. These "shades" tended to hover around their tombs or their old homes, which meant living people could placate them and perhaps get a benefit. But the shades weren't distinct personalities anymore. That's why the Romans put such great hope in being remembered on earth. If they could afford it, they erected notable tombs to honor their personal glory. The mausoleum of Emperor Hadrian, for example, looks like a giant castle in Rome today. Although various structures have been added to it over the centuries, the truth is, it was even more glorious back then than it is now.[1] Hadrian didn't want the Romans to forget him.

But even people of modest means hoped their lives would be remembered by later generations. They often built their tombs directly by the roadside, beckoning to whomever might be passing by. Consider this inscription from one Roman woman's grave:

> Stranger, I have only a few words to say. Stop and read them. This is the unlovely tomb of a lovely woman. Her parents named her Claudia. She loved her husband with all her heart. She bore two sons; one of these she leaves here on earth, the other she has already placed under the earth. She was charming in speech, yet pleasant and proper in manner. She managed the household well. She spun wool. I have spoken. Go on your way.[2]

Can you hear the longing in Claudia's voice? Since she wasn't a Christian, her hope was in remembrance of her earthly deeds. After death, she believed she would join the gloomy shades in the underworld and her personal identity would come to an end. Claudia's only hope for an afterlife was in the memories of those left behind on earth.

Ancient Christianity was exactly the opposite. It offered a personal, embodied afterlife that lasted forever—a precious promise that was one

---

1. Today it is called the Castel Sant'Angelo.

2. Shelton, *As the Romans Did*, 45.

of the main reasons for the faith's rapid growth. The Christians buried their dead individually because they expected them to rise again and be clothed in glorified flesh.

Even the poor were given spaces in the catacombs. Normally, the corpse of an impoverished person or slave would be thrown into foul garbage pits outside the city. In life, they were mistreated; in death, regarded as trash. But not so the Christians! Their gravestones were marked with a means of personal identification, for their story wasn't over yet. The dying believer looked forward to—and their loved ones took comfort in—the hope of a future bodily resurrection. Christians knew that Jesus' resurrection was a "firstfruits," that is, the initial portion of a great harvest to follow. "But each in turn," Paul wrote. "Christ, the firstfruits; then, when he comes, those who belong to him" (1 Corinthians 15:23). The risen Christ is coming back for his people. That is hope indeed!

The City of God

The church father who had the most to say about our heavenly destiny was Augustine of Hippo, whose monumental book *City of God* is one of the greatest works in world literature. Augustine wrote that all people are divided into two metaphorical cities, each centered on what they love. The earthly city loves itself, so narcissism and selfishness are the only possible outcomes. But the city of God loves him, leading to peace, happiness, wisdom, and true justice instead of constant greed and competition. All redeemed people, as well as the unfallen angels, belong to this eternal city.

For a while, though, the citizens of God's city must live down here in the earthly one. This has important ramifications for how we should view the Christian life. Every believer is a traveler, a pilgrim on a journey. And the pilgrimage is difficult. Augustine's concept of the pilgrim wasn't the happy vacationer who enjoys being on holiday. Rather, the traveler is like someone on a difficult business trip in a foreign land. This person labors for their cause even while they long to be in their true home.

What this means, in practical terms, is that the future city of God must define our present reality. Though we await a heavenly destiny, we aren't there yet. For now, we are "alien sojourners" who understand what the beauty and justice of our eternal city is like. Divine revelation has given us a glimpse of its glory. Until we get there, we will do our best to bring its splendors to our current home. By no means will we abandon the earthly city and gaze into the sky, awaiting a future rescue. Rather, we will invest deeply into the earthly city, precisely so we can lead more people out of it.

Of course, while we do love our temporary city, we cannot put our final hopes in it. Augustine knew this very well. He wrote *City of God* to explain why barbarian invaders had just sacked Rome for the first time in eight hundred years. Augustine reminds both ancient and modern believers that no earthly city was meant to last forever—not Rome, nor any city in our world today. Only the city of God is eternal.

And what will we find when we finally reach it? Augustine closes his enormous book with these glorious words: "God will be the goal of all our desires—he whom we will behold without reaching the limit, love without growing full, and praise without getting tired. This, indeed, will be our gift, our delight, our activity. And like eternal life itself, it will be shared by us all."[3]

The Fires of Hell

Not everyone, of course, reaches the heavenly city. Apart from Jesus Christ, people are lost, and their sins earn them punishment when they die. The ancient Christians believed wholeheartedly in the reality of hell. It wasn't a symbol but a real place where the wicked went after death. The teaching of Jesus on hell was too clear to be denied. It is a "blazing furnace, where there will be weeping and gnashing of teeth" (Matthew 13:42).

Despite their firm belief in hell, the church fathers weren't united on how long it might last. It's hard to find any clear doctrinal statements

---

3. *City of God* 22.30.

about this topic because many ancient writers weren't sure what to think. Yet one theme that some of them expressed was that hell's purpose is remedial. Its fires are intended to correct the wicked rather than punish them. In this way of thinking, hellfire is like the furnace of a metalsmith who smelts or refines metal to remove impurities. A scripture that was believed to support this view is 1 Corinthians 3:11-15, which speaks of God's fire of testing. Some human works are like precious metals which survive the fire, while others are burnt up like hay and straw. Paul says that some people "will suffer loss but yet will be saved—even though only as one escaping through the flames" (v. 15).

This ancient perception of hell developed in later times into the Roman Catholic doctrine of purgatory. Although the church fathers didn't go quite that far, they did seem to think that hell could sometimes be escaped. It was an eternal punishment for those who stayed unrepentant; yet those who were refined by its fires might be "saved… through the flames" as Paul described. A few church fathers like Origen of Alexandria and Gregory of Nyssa even believed that everyone would eventually repent, leading to universal salvation. While the majority of the fathers rejected that view, they left a window open to the impermanence of hell for some people.

What about that famous statement in the Apostles' Creed, "he descended into hell"? Did Jesus really go to hell between his death and resurrection? Personally, I believe this is a solid, biblical doctrine (though not every Christian today will agree with me). The important thing to recognize is that the church fathers didn't think Jesus was going to hell to suffer for sins. God's price for sin is death, and Jesus paid it in full when he said "It is finished" and died upon the cross (John 19:30; Romans 6:23). He didn't need to go to hell to suffer a little more.

Yet there are Bible passages that seem to teach that Jesus went to the underworld after he died. One of the clearest statements came from his own lips: "The Son of Man will be three days and three nights in the heart of the earth" (Matthew 12:40; see also Acts 2:27; Romans 10:7). This didn't mean a small grave near the surface, covered by a rolled stone. Jesus was referring to the sign of Jonah, who was cast into the watery abyss and was swallowed by a monster of death, yet came back from oblivion again. Why would Jesus go down to the monstrous underworld? One answer would be to proclaim in Satan's own lair that he was utterly defeated. First Peter 3:19 says that "he went and made proclamation to the imprisoned spirits." The ancient Christians believed Jesus proclaimed his triumph over the devil, then was raised from the grave. This was the glorious Christus Victor theme that we explored in chapter 1.[4]

Thy Kingdom Come

What is the relationship of God's eternal city to the physical landscape of our present earth? The ancient church's thinking about this topic changed over time. The earliest generations of church fathers believed the kingdom of Jesus would be on this earth and would last for a thousand years as described in Revelation 20. Later, following the lead of Origen and especially Augustine, the church fathers switched to a symbolic view of that Bible chapter, which meant the future kingdom of Jesus would be more of a celestial reality than something happening on our present planet. This became the majority view in church history, though the earlier view of a literal millennium that precedes the new heavens and earth still has its advocates (and I'm one of them).

Of course, Christians today can agree to disagree about the exact nature of the kingdom so long as we all acknowledge that Jesus is coming back and will reign as King. In the glorious city of God (in whatever form it takes), the resurrected Lord will be worshiped by physical people like you and me. Jesus isn't going to rule over ghosts, spirits, or disembodied souls. Nor will his subjects be humans who have been turned into angels—a doctrine never taught in Scripture nor by any respectable figure in church history.

As Christians, our destiny instead is to receive new bodies when the final trumpet sounds. We will be "raised imperishable" (1 Corinthians 15:52). Then, joined by all who have been redeemed by the blood of the

---

4. Many church fathers thought that Satan's defeat included Christ freeing Old Testament believers from the devil's captivity (Ephesians 4:8-10). I do not think, however, that this is a biblical idea.

Lamb, as well as innumerable hosts of angels, we will add our voices to the shout that is even now being heard in the throne room of God: "To him who sits on the throne and to the Lamb be praise and honor and glory and power, for ever and ever!" (Revelation 5:13). May we utter such praises with our earthly lips until the day arrives when we can say them face-to-face with the risen Christ!

> *Our citizenship is in heaven, and from it we await*
> *a Savior, the Lord Jesus Christ, who will transform*
> *our lowly body to be like his glorious body.*
>
> PHILIPPIANS 3:20-21 ESV

Conclusion

In the year 410, the warlord Alaric and his Visigothic army invaded and looted the city of Rome. A foreign enemy hadn't sacked the Eternal City since the Celts did it in 390 BC—exactly eight hundred years earlier. Alaric's momentous victory over Rome's legions marked the beginning of the end for the Roman Empire. By 476, the last emperor in the Western half of the empire had been replaced by a Germanic chieftain. Meanwhile, over in the East, what was left of the Roman Empire was well on its way to morphing into what we call the Byzantine Empire. For the sake of round numbers, we can say that the ancient Greco-Roman world ended in the year 500. Now the transition to the Middle Ages had begun.

Consider what the early Christians achieved in the first five hundred years after the birth of Jesus. They withstood the fires of persecution until imperial favor came to them at last. They stamped out heresies like Gnosticism, Marcionism, and Arianism. They clarified which books belong in the canon of Scripture. They elevated the status of women from objects of abuse to heroines of great dignity. They formulated creeds whose words were so theologically precise that we still use them today. They forged a new architecture of unique beauty and timeless appeal. They evangelized not only the vast empire but the heathen people beyond. They bequeathed to later generations the proper language to speak about the Trinity and Christology. And through all this, they showed the world that the Jewish carpenter whom the Romans had executed was actually the victorious Savior of humankind. The foundations of Christianity were now in place. The church was ready to face its next thousand years.

One of the church fathers who witnessed the passing of the ancient world into the medieval was Augustine of Hippo. After an immoral and impious beginning to his life, he had converted dramatically to the Lord and embarked on four decades of fruitful ministry. But as his life was coming to a close, the stable, unified world he had always known was also coming to an end. To the west of Hippo, a horde of Germanic invaders—this time, the Vandals—had crossed the sea from Spain and were sweeping across North Africa, leaving devastation in their wake. The Christians of Hippo cowered behind their walls as they found their city surrounded and besieged.

Though this looming terror would afflict Augustine's flock, the man himself would escape the violence and vandalism to come. At 75 years old, he was on the verge of death. How did this great bishop spend his final days? While his strength lasted, he kept on preaching sermons and exhorting his flock to persevere. But finally he grew too weak to continue, so he took to his bed.

And then what did he do? Augustine's biographer tells us that he commanded the penitential psalms to be written on sheets and hung on the walls around his bed.[1] For ten days, Augustine remained totally alone except when receiving food or care. In the silence of that little room, while the Vandal horde clamored outside the city walls, the greatest of the church fathers repented of his sins and communed with God by reading the Word. To me, this poignant image of Augustine's spiritual desire symbolizes—more than any mighty deed, great doctrine, or landmark event in church history—why the ancient Christians deserve to be heard today.

I would like to close this book by offering you one of the psalms that Augustine read on his deathbed as the earthly city faded from him and

---

1. Possidius, *Life of Augustine* 31.

the city of God began to shine upon his soul. I hope you will forgive me, but I have slightly adapted the final verses of Psalm 130 (ESV) so you may receive the psalm's words personally and apply them to yourself. Perhaps Augustine did the same in ancient Hippo as he read these words on his way to heaven:

> Out of the depths I cry to you, O LORD!
>
> Lord, hear my voice!
> Let your ears be attentive to the voice
> of my pleas for mercy!
>
> If you, O LORD, should mark iniquities,
> O Lord, who could stand?
> But with you there is forgiveness,
> that you may be feared.
>
> I wait for the LORD, my soul waits,
> and in his word do I hope;
> my soul waits for the Lord
> more than watchmen for the morning,
> more than watchmen for the morning.
>
> O Christian, hope in the LORD!
> For with the LORD there is steadfast love,
> with him there is plentiful redemption.
> And he will redeem you from all your iniquities.
> And all God's people said:
> *Amen!*

About the Author

Bryan Litfin has a ThM in historical theology from Dallas Seminary and a PhD in ancient Christianity from the University of Virginia. He is the author of several books and scholarly articles on the early church, as well as six published or forthcoming novels (three of which are set in the ancient church era). Bryan lives with his wife and two children in Illinois, where he is the Head of Strategy and Advancement at Clapham School, a classical Christian school. For more about him, see his website at BryanLitfin.com.

To learn more about Harvest House books and
to read sample chapters, visit our website:

www.harvesthousepublishers.com

HARVEST HOUSE PUBLISHERS
EUGENE, OREGON